TWAYNE'S WORLD AUTHORS SERIES
A Survey of the World's Literature

GERMANY

Ulrich Weisstein, Indiana University

EDITOR

Conrad Ferdinand Meyer

TWAS 480

Conrad Ferdinand Meyer

CONRAD FERDINAND MEYER

By MARIANNE BURKHARD
University of Illinois at Urbana-Champaign

TWAYNE PUBLISHERS
A DIVISION OF G. K. HALL & CO., BOSTON

Library of Congress Cataloging in Publication Data

Burkhard, Marianne.
    Conrad Ferdinand Meyer.

    (Twayne's world authors series ; TWAS 480 : Germany)
    Bibliography: P. 167–71
    Includes index.
    1. Meyer, Conrad Ferdinand, 1825–1898 — Criticism and in-
terpretation.
PT2432.Z9B84   1978   831'.7   77–28441
ISBN 0–8057–6321–X

It is not what a lawyer tells me I *may* do;
but what humanity, reason, and justice, tell
me I ought to do.

Edmund Burke

*This book is dedicated to my friends in the
United States.*

Contents

About the Author

Marianne Burkhard received her education from the University of Zurich, the University of Hamburg and at the Sorbonne in Paris. She received her Ph.D. in 1965 from the University of Zurich, with a major in modern German literature and a minor in French literature. From 1965 to 1968 she served as the Literary Editor of *Zurichsee-Zeitung* (daily). She was awarded an assistant professorship of German at the University of Illinois in 1968 and today holds the title of Associate Professor of German at the University of Illinois.

Marianne Burkhard has previously had published three books and seven articles. The books include a published dissertation, *C.F. Meyer und die Antike Mythologie* and two other books which she edited, *Fruchtbringender Lustgarte* and *Gottfried Keller-Vom Maler zum Dichter*. Reviews of her work have appeared in several scholarly journals. She is also listed in *The World's Who is Who of Women*, 3d ed., 1976 and *Who's Who of American Women*, 10th ed., 1977–78.

Preface

Within German literature of the later nineteenth century the Swiss writer Conrad Ferdinand Meyer occupies a distinguished place even though his work, written between 1870 and 1891, is limited in size. He is best known for his historical novellas in which he conjures up figures of the great European past from the Middle Ages to the seventeenth century. A master of colorful images and concise, dramatic form, Meyer raised the historical novella — a popular genre at the time — to new artistic heights. His poetry comprises historical ballads as well as delicate lyric poems. In the latter he explored, and sometimes brought to perfection, new modes of poetic expression which were ahead of contemporary German poetry. Thus Meyer's work as a whole eludes any single stylistic designation.

The difficulty of categorizing Meyer is reflected in the ways he has been viewed. During his lifetime and in the first half of the twentieth century he was considered as a clear representative of the conservative bourgeois attitudes dominant in Germany between 1870 and 1890. This period following the founding of the German Empire is now commonly called the Founders' Era (*Gründerzeit*). Finally unified under Emperor Wilhelm I, Germany enjoyed an unprecedented prosperity. Bismarck's politics and the victory in the Franco-Prussian War of 1870–1871 provided the young empire with great political power. Expansion of all industries brought economic prosperity to the country and especially to the upper middle class. Consequently, traditional bourgeois values were reinforced; individual success, political power, and moral stature were admired and often fused into a vision of heroic greatness. Though Swiss, Meyer knew this world well; and in his novellas he wanted to address the educated bourgeois readers in Germany as well as those in Switzerland.

After 1945, however, some scholars have given special attention to Meyer's lyrics which do not fit the stylistic ideals of the *Gründerzeit* and which were, therefore, long underestimated. These studies, pioneered by Heinrich Henel, show Meyer as a poetic innovator marking the transition from the confessional, openly personal poetry of the classical-romantic tradition, to modern poetry in which subjective content is transmitted in an indirect way through more objective imagery and less emotional language. In this respect Meyer evinces affinities with French symbolism in the vein of Charles Baudelaire and Stéphane Mallarmé. Recognizing this modern facet of Meyer's poetry has actually paved the way for a better assessment of his work. A thorough examination reveals that his historical novellas, too, are interfused with modern insights and with unconventional interpretations of *Gründerzeit* conventions.

The present study, the first monograph of Meyer's life and his entire work in English, shows him as the transitional figure he is. The general and specific conditions of his life placed him between times and styles: he is no longer a true *Gründerzeit* author nor is he yet a full-blooded symbolist, a truly modern writer. It is this very ambivalence in style and attitude that distinguished him from the average *Gründerzeit* author and prompted him to create works which continue to fascinate modern readers.

All of Meyer's prose works are now accessible in new English translations by George F. Folkers, David B. Dickens, and Marion W. Sonnenfeld. Since only a few novellas were previously available, often in very old translations, only the new translations, published in two volumes in 1976, are mentioned in the bibliography. The translations from Meyer's prose and his letters in this study are, however, my own; Dr. Janette C. Hudson (Charlottesville, Virginia) contributed the bulk of the poetry translations. Wherever possible I have indicated the chapter in which a specific passage is found in order to make it easier to locate that passage either in the translation or in a German edition other than the historical-critical Meyer edition.

In closing, I would like to thank my friends Janette C. Hudson, Harold Jantz (Duke University), and Philip E. Grundlehner (University of Illinois) who have generously given their time to read over my manuscript and to discuss specific translation problems. I also wish to thank the University of Illinois at Urbana-Champaign for having granted me a sabbatical leave for 1976–1977.

MARIANNE BURKHARD
University of Illinois at Urbana-Champaign

Chronology

1875 October 5, marries Luise Ziegler.
1876 Publishes *Jürg Jenatsch* in book form.
1877 Purchases home in Kilchberg; *Der Schuss von der Kanzel.*
1879 *Der Heilige,* published, like all but one of the following novellas, in *Die Deutsche Rundschau.*
1881 *Plautus im Nonnenkloster.*
1882 *Gedichte; Gustav Adolfs Page.*
1883 *Das Leiden eines Knaben* published in *Schorers Familienblatt; Die Hochzeit des Mönchs.*
1885 *Die Richterin.*
1887 *Die Versuchung des Pescara.*
1888 Long illness (January to October).
1891 *Angela Borgia.*
1892 Confinement in Königsfelden (July).
1893 Return to Kilchberg (September).
1898 November 28, Meyer dies in his home in Kilchberg.

CHAPTER 1

Conrad Ferdinand Meyer's Life

CONRAD Ferdinand Meyer's life is unusual, and the course of his literary career intriguing. He was born on October 11, 1825, in Zurich, Switzerland, and died on November 28, 1898, in Kilchberg, a few miles from there. Although his life spans three-quarters of a century, all his major works were written in the short period between 1870 and 1892. By this circumstance alone, Meyer stands out against the vast majority of modern writers with whose lives we are familiar: they start writing early, are most prolific in youth and maturity, and often become less productive with advancing age. Meyer's case seems even more unusual when we consider the fact that from very early on he wanted to be a poet, that he was not trained for any profession and never held a regular full-time job which might have impaired his creativity. The reasons for such a singular development are complex, stemming from problems inherent in Meyer's psyche, his family and his social environment, and his situation in a time of changing literary style.

A presentation of Meyer's life and work can be divided into two parts: the long period of preparation (from 1825 to 1869) and the short creative period (from 1870 to 1892). This temporal division brings with it a shift in emphasis: in the first chapter, covering the slow formation of the writer, biographical data will prevail, while Chapters 2 to 8 will focus mainly on Meyer's work, since in this time of artistic accomplishment his biography becomes much less significant.

I *Spell-bound in a Dream (1825–1856)*

At the time of Meyer's birth, Zurich was a small city surrounded by fortifications complete with walls, bulwarks, moats, and gates.

13

For a brief period — the post-Napoleonic restoration (1814–1830) — the city's aristocracy was again in firm control of the city and the cantonal government. However, in the 1820s, this conservative system no longer went completely unchallenged. Younger members of the ruling Zurich families started to voice a moderate liberal opposition by advocating a free press and some judicial reforms. Meyer's father, Ferdinand, belonged to this group. Outside the city, in Zurich's rural district the discontent was much stronger, the call for changes louder, since, after 1814, the city had again assumed absolute dominance in the cantonal government as well as in other important political offices.[1]

The 1830 July Revolution in Paris precipitated this change. Backed by a growing number of mass meetings, the rural politicians forced the city to agree to a new constitution and to direct elections for the cantonal government (Great Council). In 1831, the newly elected Great Council had a radical-democratic majority, and by 1832 radicals also prevailed in the Small Council. Because of this abrupt change, Ferdinand Meyer, despite his basically liberal ideas, found himself aligned with the moderate conservatives, and in 1832 he resigned his seat in the radicalized Small Council. This shift in politics occasioned a series of important changes in Zurich: the fortifications, the symbol of the city's dominance, were dismantled, the old city privileges abolished, and the university was founded (1833) at which renowned German and Swiss scholars taught. The fact that in 1836 the university offered Georg Büchner a position as lecturer shows the liberal spirit of this young institution. Thus, Zurich opened to the changing world: it allowed cooperation with the surrounding rural district on the political and economic level and participated in the exchange of philosophical and scientific ideas through its university.

In 1839, however, this very open-mindedness provoked a counterrevolution. With a narrow victory, the radicals appointed the controversial David Friedrich Strauss as professor of theology. The conservatives, together with the mostly orthodox church, violently opposed this nomination, and after the short Zurich Riot (*Zürcher Putsch,* on September 6, 1839), they swept the radicals out of office. Again, Ferdinand Meyer occupied a high post in the conservative government. Only three years later the conservatives lost half of their seats, and until 1848 Zurich as well as the other Swiss cantons were plagued by turbulent disorder culminating in the Civil War of 1847 (*Sonderbundskrieg*). The creation of a more unified state based on the federal constitution of 1848 marked the beginning of a more peaceful era.

This cursory glance at history outlines the radical changes wrought upon Zurich in the 1830s. Although Meyer was just a boy then, he had — according to his sister Betsy[2] — an early interest in politics; the manifold attacks on traditional values and established systems, and the ensuing atmosphere of general instability, affected his view of the world in a significant way. In all of his works, except in *Engelberg,* Meyer portrays a world in the midst of changes which are at once desired and abhorred. Again and again his thoughts center around the phenomena of a tradition seriously questioned and of an established order disintegrating because of inner weaknesses. This feeling of instability has yet another facet — a growing sense of the relativity of positions and attitudes whose significance could be suddenly and basically changed by a political shift.

At the time of his baptism, Meyer received the name of his maternal grandfather Conrad. When he started publishing poems in literary journals in 1865, he added his father's name Ferdinand so as not to be mistaken for another writer of the region by the name of Konrad Meyer.[3] After having gained a reputation as a writer under his double first name, Meyer had it legalized in 1877.

Meyer's sister Betsy describes their childhood as happy, protected, and carefree.[4] In many ways Meyer and his sister were indeed fortunate. They lived with their parents and their maternal grandmother in a large house with a spacious garden. Although Ferdinand Meyer was not rich, he could offer his family a comfortable life, and his social position, his interests, and relations enabled him to provide his children with an intellectually stimulating environment. Ferdinand Meyer (1799–1840) was not only a politician but also an historian who liked to entertain his children with stories about the old Greeks, the Romans, and the Germans.[5] In his spare time he wrote a highly regarded *History of the Protestant Community of Locarno*[6] for which the University of Zurich awarded him an honorary doctoral degree. His wife, Betsy (Elisabeth) Ulrich (1802–1856), possessed a lively imagination, perspicacity coupled with charm, and the gift of an accomplished hostess. Politicians as well as university professors met regularly in Meyer's hospitable home, and these intellectual gatherings produced an atmosphere which transcended the rather narrow horizon of a provincial city in the 1830s. In the summers of 1836 and 1838 Ferdinand Meyer undertook hiking trips with his son; he introduced him to the rich historical world of the canton Graubünden which would later play such an important role in his son's thinking and writing. Thus, in his early life the boy enjoyed the immense advantages of a cultured and stimulating environment.

At the same time, this environment had its serious drawbacks, which must have affected Meyer from the time he was a very young boy. His mother was subject to depressions caused by highly irritable and overdelicate nerves. Aware of this hereditary condition she countered it with self-discipline and, more importantly, with a deep religious belief. A rather melancholy outlook on life characterized the young mother. In her earnest devotion she stressed guilt and self-abasement, elements not conducive to a free evolution of her son's artistic talents.

Difficulties in Conrad's development first became evident when, at the age of six, his nature underwent a drastic change: the lively and good-tempered child became listless and irritable, was at times stubborn and at other times pliable. Meyer's biographers attribute this change mainly to a bout of roseola which befell the child in 1831. Psychologically oriented studies interpret it either in a strict Freudian manner as the result of awakening erotic interests which distracted the boy from all other things,[7] or as the boy's reaction to the birth of his sister Betsy in 1831.[8] The interpretation of this change is further complicated by the fact that, from Betsy's birth on, Conrad took an extraordinary fancy to his sister. Due to the scarcity of the reports a final explanation of the change is very difficult; however, it is important to note the phenomenon, since it shows how precarious the balance in Meyer's physical and psychological nature was from the outset.

In the light of this circumstance, it is no wonder that the death of Ferdinand Meyer in 1840 had a deeply disturbing effect on his fifteen-year-old son. Although Ferdinand Meyer spent little time with his children, he was engaged in writing and interpreting history and, therefore, might have had a genuine understanding for Conrad's literary aspirations. In the family, he displayed a natural gaiety which was a welcome complement to the more serious attitude of his wife.

According to reliable sources, Conrad did not show visible signs of grief at or after his father's death. In this, a most characteristic trait of his nature comes to the fore: his seeming impassiveness in the face of an unusual impression or experience. During his entire life, his external behavior does not provide direct clues to the depth of his feelings. However, over the years following his father's death Conrad became more irascible, vacillating between physical hyperactivity and intellectual indolence. Unfortunately, his mother was ill prepared to cope with such erratic behavior. She had lost the vital emotional support which her husband had given her and which had allowed her to confront problems with less anxiety. Since self-discipline and a firm Christian belief were her chief defense in the difficulties of life, she could interpret her son's behavior only in terms of deliberate, un-Christian arrogance. Therefore, she was unable to grasp, under the sometimes rebellious surface, Conrad's deep insecurity which led him either to attack the world or to withdraw from it in self-protection. His first poems[9] written in these years mirror this: he is preoccupied with thunderstorm and battle metaphors as well as with the thought of death and its calm.

In 1843, Mrs. Meyer decided that a separation of Conrad from her as well as from his unruly classmates in the Zurich Gymnasium was necessary. Conrad welcomed the idea of spending a year in Lausanne in the French-speaking part of Switzerland, where his family had many friends. This change affected him immediately in a positive way. Freed from the school he disliked, he avidly read Jean Paul, Alfred de Musset, and the French classics. He enjoyed meeting unusual people such as the well-known historian Louis Vulliemin, the mystical painter Melchior Paul Deschwanden, Polish refugees, and his Italian teacher, who was full of revolutionary ideas. Lausanne was thus an experience of freedom and self-assertion: in a long poem entitled "Lake Leman" he urges the lake, which a remark to his sister likens to his own breast, to give up its slavelike calm and to show its full force by breaking its shackles.

Important as this experience was, it could not help him to surmount the confining conditions at home. Back in Zurich in 1844, he passed his final school examination and complied with his mother's wish that he study law and follow in his father's footsteps. In the absence of a real inclination or, at least, a decision of his own, Meyer soon began to drift and to withdraw into his own world of reading, writing and, for a while, drawing — a world which was even more private for the lack of guidance. The two instances of direct guidance which he received — most probably in the winter of 1844-1845 — only enhanced his insecurity. One involved his work with a painter; it soon became clear to him that his talent would not suffice for a painting career. The second instance was more disturbing: Meyer's mother asked the Swabian writer Gustav Pfizer[10] for an evaluation of Conrad's poems. Anticipating a positive judgment she put Pfizer's unopened letter on the Christmas tree; this well-meant surprise aggravated the shock of Pfizer's advice that Meyer should abandon poetry and become a painter. Pfizer's judgment is understandable, since these poems often show an awkward language, forced rhymes, and unpolished imagery. For the Meyer scholar, however, they are extremely interesting for their content which should be analyzed in detail.[11] Two recurring motifs seem essential: the motif of a tree or a rock which, after a raging storm, appear not just unharmed but even stronger. But this positive view of difficulties is contrasted by the wish for death, the image of a misjudged genius and, more strikingly, by a poem "Epitaphe" describing a dead poet who was unable to realize his talent because he was out of step with the surrounding world. This poet bears Meyer's own traits, and thus the poem is a masked expression of his deep fear that he might never succeed in achieving recognition as the poet he felt himself to be.

The rejection of his poetic endeavors by a professional writer and, consequently, by his mother was a hard blow to which Meyer could only react by withdrawing into his own world. This withdrawal became a permanent condition turning, as the years went by, into an ever deepening isolation not broken until 1852 when Meyer sought psychiatric help in the clinic of Préfargier near Neuchâtel. Although we have little precise information about the time between 1845 and 1852, an analysis of certain factors in Meyer's situation can shed some light on its complexity. Pfizer's letter must have had a contradictory effect on Meyer. It enhanced his insecurity concerning his poetic talent and, at the same time, it must have strengthened his desire to be a poet because it confronted him with the prospect of a life without poetry — a prospect which probably made him feel how vitally important writing was for him. In addition, Pfizer's judgment led Meyer to doubt whether true communication about poetry was possible; therefore, he did not make another attempt to get advice; he continued to work on his own, seeking no stimulation from outside.

And this outside world did not offer stimulation to the young poet. In the nineteenth century, Zurich had lost the rich literary life which had been its mark in the second half of the preceding century, in the time when Bodmer and Breitinger took such an important part in the discussion of literary theory, when Salomon Gessner enchanted an European public with his idyls, when Bodmer and Lavater attracted such distinguished visitors as Klopstock, Wieland, and the young Goethe. However, Zurich had no younger writers to carry on such a literary life. Thus, after 1800, the city slipped back into provinciality. Zurich's new development, beginning in the 1830s, was primarily due to the expansion of business and industry, while the new intellectual climate promoted by the founding of the university followed the trend of the time toward the exact sciences. In the 1840s, the German writers Georg Herwegh and Ferdinand Freiligrath stayed for a while in Zurich. But for them, its attraction was not that of a literary city, but of a refuge from the persecution they experienced in their dictatorial German states, which disapproved of their expressed political views. Herwegh's and Freiligrath's stays were short and their experiences and thinking quite foreign, so that they could neither have a sizable influence nor revive a literary life. The fact that Zurich had become so much a city of commerce exerted yet another negative influence on Meyer's development. In an atmosphere determined by practical efficiency he was considered more and more an odd figure. His goal of a poetic career was, in the opinion of the bourgeoisie, a frivolous endeavor and not a serious task for life. Meyer was keenly aware of such disapproval and of what was expected from him as the son of a man who had embodied the Protestant work ethic and had been regarded as a model public servant. But Meyer had neither the strong motivation to fulfill these expectations nor the clear conviction of his poetic talent which would have enabled him to defy the expectations openly. Caught between such external demands and his internal resistance to them he retreated, even from his school friends, took walks only at night, and spent long, lonely hours swimming and rowing on the nearby lake.

At home, disapproval was evident, too, in the way his mother silently bore her disappointment caused by his inability to gain a place in the elite of Zurich's society. She also was concerned about the practical aspect of her son's idleness: the family's financial means were not such that Conrad could live comfortably without earning money. During this isolation, Meyer had only one real companion — his younger sister Betsy (1831–1912). She was the only one in which he could confide. Her youth set her apart from a disapproving society, her natural sensitivity and interest for literature allowed her to comprehend her brother's fascination with writing, and his confiding in her deepened her admiration for his plans which, to her youthful thinking, appeared full of exciting promise. Meyer shared with Betsy his writing attempts which between 1845 and 1850 consisted mainly of epic and dramatic fragments treating subjects from the history of ancient Rome (Tullia, Tarquinius) and of the Italian Renaissance (Cesare Borgia); other plans centered around the medieval German emperors, for example, Otto III and Frederick II.[12] These topics reappear in some form in poems and novellas written decades later when Meyer had fully developed his style. Thus, it was in this period of seemingly aimless experimenting that he began to grasp certain historical events around which his imagination would later crystallize.

With Betsy, Meyer also shared his reading interests which centered on the German romantic writers Tieck, Novalis, and Friedrich Schlegel, as well as on writers admired by the romantics, such as Calderón and Shakespeare. The younger generation of German writers fascinated him too: he recited Platen to Betsy, gave her the newly published poetry collections of Lenau and Freiligrath as Christmas presents,[13] and admired Herwegh, whom he later called "the poet of my youth."[14] Traditional Meyer scholarship has only stressed the romantic side of these readings which reinforced his introspective attitude and his escape into a world of fantasy and dreams. Meyer is then viewed as secluded from and untouched by the turbulent political events of the years 1844 to 1847[15] leading to the Civil War of 1847, the defeat of the conservatives, and ultimately to the creation of a radical-democratic Swiss state in 1848. However, Meyer was not as uninterested in political events as the critics would have us believe. Betsy reports that he was an avid reader of newspapers and followed the political events with interest.[16] In this light, Meyer's predilection for such political poets as Herwegh and Freiligrath and his plan to write an epic poem about the French Revolution[17] are not only understandable but indicate that the radical ideas of the years spent in Lausanne had not altogether disappeared, and that his viewpoint was, on the whole, anticonservative.[18] It is important to take this liberal orientation into account because it provides an element linking this solitary period of Meyer's life with both the Lausanne experience, when he read the works of such socialist reformers as Lammenais, and the indirect criticism leveled in his later works at closed social systems and fixed ways of thinking. The fact that even in his seclusion Meyer kept an interest in the political changes of the time suggests that he associated his own need for personal liberation with the need for changes in larger social contexts. This thought is the basis for his admiration of great individuals who break through the social conventions in order to realize their full personal potential, for example, Hutten, Jenatsch, Wertmüller, and Gustel Leubelfing. But not even political events coinciding with some of his liberal ideas could jar Meyer out of his lethargy, and this points to the seriousness of his emotional difficulties at the time. His unresponsive attitude presents also a striking contrast to the development of Gottfried Keller, whose poetic talent was roused by the political events in the 1840s.

Besides literary works Meyer read numerous historical studies, thus acquiring a broad knowledge. However, the book which most impressed him was neither a literary nor a historical but a critical work, namely, Friedrich Theodor Vischer's *Kritische Gänge* (*Critical Thrusts,* 1844). Vischer (1807–1887), by training a protestant theologian, was since 1835 professor of German literature and aesthetics at the University of Tübingen. His essays, written between 1838 and 1844, cover subjects ranging from contemporary theology (a defense of his classmate David Friedrich Strauss against Swabian Pietism), and German romantic painting to contemporary literature (Mörike and Herwegh). In a spirited manner, combining sensitivity and acumen, Vischer took issue not only with individual works but also with general phenomena characterizing German art and thinking in the 1830s and early 1840s. His main criticism concerned the prevalence of the purely spiritual outlook and the ensuing neglect of considering reality. Vischer exemplified this neglect of reality especially in the domain of romantic painting whose myths and allegories aimed at showing a timeless, general transcendence instead of historical or contemporary reality, and in the dominance of abstract concepts and rhetoric in even the political poetry of Herwegh.

According to Betsy,[19] Vischer's book struck Meyer with unexpected force. Suddenly he was confronted with an imperious and brilliantly formulated demand that realistic portrayal of the world in its present and historical forms be the core of any true art. This strong call for realism unsettled Meyer: it attacked his romantic view of literature as separated from reality and thus offering a refuge from the unpoetic everyday, and it implicitly criticized his existence in a secluded world of dreams and vague literary projects. Coming from an art expert this criticism was much more serious than that of the Zurich bourgeoisie, and Meyer must have keenly felt its justification. By destroying his romantic ideas about literature Vischer's books prepared the ground on which Meyer could slowly develop a style more in tune with his personality and his time. But the immediate effect was a deeply disturbing one, since Vischer's lucid analysis of romantic art collapsed the world which Meyer had designed for his refuge from an inimical reality. Thus, his insecurity deepened, his delicate nerves could not bear the stress, and his behavior became neurotic. He left his room less and less often and kept the shutters closed to avoid the daylight; he was convinced that he emanated a disagreeable odor and that for this reason nobody could like him; and often he was haunted by suicidal thoughts. Meyer's mother refrained from intervening, even from remonstrating, but this very passive attitude and some words Meyer happened to overhear[20] showed him that she had given up all hope of seeing her son occupy a respectable position in the world. In the spring of 1852 his physical and mental state deteriorated to the point where a separation from the family became imperative. Both mother and son recognized the need for professional help, which was sought in the clinic of Préfargier near Neuchâtel.

The choice of the clinic proved to be excellent. Its situation in the French part of Switzerland emphasized the change of scene which Meyer so urgently needed, and the use of a foreign language in discussing his difficulties provided a first, minimal distance from his intensely painful experiences. Most important was the fact that the clinic's director, Dr. James Borrel, and his sister Cécile, the head nurse, created a domestic atmosphere of kindness and understanding for the patients in general and for Meyer in particular, who was treated like a member of the Borrel family. This atmosphere as well as Borrel's prescription for manual labor in the clinic's garden and strict regularity in the daily routine provided the external change necessary for the solving of Meyer's psychological problems. The seven months Meyer spent in Préfargier, as well as the following year he spent in Neuchâtel and Lausanne, are well documented in Robert d'Harcourt's publication of letters by Meyer, Dr. James and Cécile Borrel, Meyer's mother and sister, and others.[21] These letters provide insight into Meyer's attitudes and into the conditions under which he started to reshape his life. Dr. Borrel's reports to Meyer's mother also furnish information about the patient's hallucinatory condition, the physical and psychological treatment, and his relatively rapid recovery. Despite these rather detailed accounts psychiatrists seem unable to agree on a medical definition of Meyer's illness;[22] therefore, no attempt at such a definition is made here.

Meyer's physical well-being was soon restored; the tasks of restoring his psychological balance and of developing his entire personality were more complex, and their results were not wholly satisfying. Borrel recognized that his patient needed both a prolonged separation from his mother and financial independence. Embracing these ideas Meyer planned to use his stay in Préfargier to study the French language and literature, thus preparing for a career as a teacher of French at a secondary school (gymnasium) in Germany. This gave him real hope that a brighter future with a respectable position was within his reach. However, the plan had a serious drawback since, in their Christian piety, Borrel and his associates thought it necessary for Meyer to abandon any literary endeavors. Although the people in Préfargier exhibited a more open and more optimistic Christian belief than did Meyer's mother, they, too, misinterpreted Meyer's poetic aspirations as the cause for his breakdown, as having awakened in him an impious desire for worldly success and a sinful, proud reliance on his own will. Therefore, much of the advice given to Meyer centered on his acquiring true Christian humility which would best be expressed in renouncing his old ambition of doing "something unusual and accomplished either in literature or in the arts" (*C,* 5).

This well-meant advice brought Meyer into a difficult situation. His letters show him to be keenly aware of his "miserable position in this world" (*C,* 42), of the failure of his past and of the pain caused to his family; far from being proud, he looked with "fear and trembling" (*C,* 42) into an uncertain future. He also felt deep gratitude and respect for the Borrels who had helped him to regain normal contact with the outside world. Yet the same people required him to give up the one thing which he felt to be the core and purpose of his life — his writing plans. Their importance is suggested in the following statement reported by Dr. Borrel: "To attain this goal [of creating something accomplished] I have striven to develop in me the understanding and the feeling for the beautiful, the only goods I appreciate in this world" (*C,* 5). Having no proof yet of his talent and feeling deeply humiliated by his status as a mental patient, Meyer was in no position to rebel; thus, he yielded to the advice of seeking nothing but a simple teaching career. However, the tenacity with which he pursued his writing suggests that this renouncement was actually a temporary, therapeutic measure rather than a permanent decision. Consciously or unconsciously, this behavior includes a certain diplomacy which Meyer once described to Betsy by saying that he was inclined to follow necessity because this made less noise than manifesting a free will (*C*, 115). It is no accident that he made this remark in connection with an instance of exaggerated piety. For whenever confronted with admonitions to become a better, that is, humbler Christian, he assumed a certain sincere but limited compliance which guaranteed him some privacy and freedom in the formulation of his personal faith. It seems that in this position between two opposite forces Meyer instinctively developed an attitude which allowed him to accept Borrel's advice while keeping a mental reserve to protect his most private thoughts. As we will see, this diplomatic attitude assumed by the weak vis-à-vis the more powerful is not only typical for Meyer's personal behavior, but also becomes an important feature of his work.

Summarizing the effects of Meyer's stay in Préfargier, two points are to be noted. On the one hand, the stay was successful in helping him to find his way back to the outside world. A tender but never fully declared affection for Cécile Borrel brought about an awakening of his emotional life which Dr. Borrel had seen as an essential element for recovery. The stability and confidence he had gained in Préfargier soon withstood an unexpected test when, in early 1853, he spent two months in the home of Professor Godet in Neuchâtel. There he was exposed to an austere religious atmosphere — a stark contrast to Préfargier — and to Godet's stern remonstrances that his entire way of thinking was wrong. It is to the credit of both doctor and patient that Meyer was able to handle this situation in a mature manner. On the other hand, Préfargier could not deal with his problem of how to realize his artistic potential. But at least they supported his study of French literature as a preparation for a career. Thus, they encouraged a secondary contact with the world of writing, while his mother would have preferred that he completely abandon the realm of books and ideas which she considered to be his greatest danger. Still, any real development of Meyer's writing potential was again — as in Zurich — constricted by the limited views of his immediate environment.

This changed when, in March, 1853, Meyer left Neuchâtel and went to Lausanne for further French studies. There, he was again welcomed to the circle of Louis Vulliemin. Vulliemin assumed the role of Meyer's mentor with natural discretion and a rare intuition for both Meyer's as yet unrealized potential and his past frustrations. He discerned that his young friend was in need of some definite project which would require active work — not just passive studying — and would produce tangible results. Within a few weeks he had him working on a German translation of a book by the French historian Augustin Thierry's *Tales from the Times of the Merovingians,* and later he procured him an assignment to teach history at the Lausanne Institute for the Blind. The work as teacher and translator fulfilled crucial functions for Meyer: after years of idling he was forced to work steadily, thus experiencing, for the first time in his adult life, the satisfaction of regularly performed intellectual work. Both projects provided him with an intense contact with history whose material — rich in characters and events — stimulated his imagination. The translation presented him with an opportunity to work with the German language in a new way: he had to subject his creativity to the discipline of precisely rendering an already created text. Instead of pursuing an elusive inspiration and producing only disjointed fragments — as he had done in Zurich — he now had to apply himself diligently to the more modest problems of re-creating the nuances of Thierry's language in German. In a letter to Mrs. Meyer, Vulliemin wrote: "... he works ... slowly but perseveringly; he struggles desirous of creating a work of art and [he is], if I may judge from what I have heard [of the translation] capable of succeding" (*C*, 164). This description is significant, since it points out that Meyer was learning to persevere and to recognize the importance of even the small details in artistic creation — elements which are not only characteristic of his way of writing but essential for his eventual success.

By translating Meyer gained confidence in himself, because his work met with the approval of Vulliemin who was both a translator and a historical writer of distinction.[23] For the first time, Meyer could profit from the close contact with someone who sensed his artistic potential and was able to provide him with some guidance. He also became more confident in his social contacts: he associated with other young men, passed for an interesting conversationalist who did not fail to impress a couple of young ladies, and his letters often showed sparks of wit. His growing emotional stability also manifested itself in the new way Meyer related to the two women who had played a decisive role in his recent past: Cécile Borrel and his mother. When writing to Cécile he now felt secure enough to hint delicately at the sentiments he had harbored for her. In the letters to his mother equanimity and understanding replaced his earlier, quickly roused irritation. This is all the more remarkable in view of the fact that she kept reminding him of such petty details as to tidy up his room, to account for every penny spent, and not to wipe his razor with a handkerchief. Increasingly, Mrs. Meyer also felt compelled to accuse herself of having caused her son's breakdown, an accusation which he tried to refute by expressing his firm conviction that his illness was the result of his physical constitution. At the time when he began to act independently, her criticism and depression grew, indicating that, subconsciously, she needed her son's dependence on her.

At the end of 1853 Meyer returned to Zurich without having achieved the external goals of finding a job and gaining financial independence. But he had made essential internal progress; for he was now able to cope with the demands of living at home — with his mother's indirect but always noticeable criticism of both his literary interests and his lack of Christian fervor and with the fact that, in the eyes of the Zurich society, he was still a failure. He continued to work steadily on the last revision of his Thierry translation, which was published anonymously in 1855.[24] Thus, at the age of thirty, Meyer received a first recognition of his work in the form of publication and of a modest honorarium. Next he translated Guizot's *L'Amour dans le mariage* which was published in 1857 under the title *Lady Russel: Eine geschichtliche Studie* (*Lady Russel: An Historical Study*).[25] Yet Meyer's life was still rather aimless except for the one purpose about which he dared not say much — a writing career. A passage from a letter to his friend Vulliemin captures his mood at this time: "I am living only for my work [his translations], I like it and I am not worried about the rest.... nobody will ever take away my pen; — I would like to be capable of better things and to contribute a bit of my own; perhaps this will come later, patience!"[26] In 1856 this quiet life came to an end when Antonin Mallet, the long-time housemate of the Meyer family, died. He was a mentally retarded member of an aristocratic Geneva family and had spent most of his life in the care of Mrs. Meyer's parents and of Mrs. Meyer herself. With his death, Mrs. Meyer lost a responsibility which, after Conrad's recovery, had become the center of her self-sacrificing life. Thus, her depression was aggravated to the point where she had to be taken to Préfargier; and on September 27, 1856, she drowned herself. Though grieved and shaken by guilt after his mother's death, Meyer also felt relieved from the pressure of the ever-conflicting relationship with his mother. Without the burden of her constant doubts and rigid demands he was now free to concentrate on writing. At the same time, he was freed from any financial worries, since Antonin Mallet had bequeathed a considerable sum to Conrad and Betsy; this money allowed them to lead a modestly comfortable life without having to work.

II *Encounter with the World (1857–1858)*

Looking at Meyer's life after 1856 we realize what an impact his new independence had on his general attitude toward life. In 1857 and 1858 he undertook three journeys: to Paris (March to June, 1857), to Munich (October, 1857), and to Rome and Florence (March to June, 1858). These travels indicate Meyer's desire to see the world, about which he had only read, and to face life outside his imagination. The opening poem of the cycle "Travel" contains the lines: "Ich war von einem schweren Bann gebunden. / Ich lebte nicht. Ich lag im Traum erstarrt" ("I was bound by an oppressive spell. / I did not live. Torpid, I lay in a dream"). This is contrasted with the refrain: "Tag, schein herein und, Leben, flieh hinaus!" ("Day, shine in and life, flow outside!"). The spell of introversion was now broken. The new openness enabled Meyer to absorb what he saw with such precision and intensity that even two and three decades later his travel impressions served him as vivid material for his works. Thus, despite the relative shortness of these trips, they represent a significant formative stage in the shaping of his poetic world.

While in Paris, Meyer described his impressions in letters to Betsy which Frey quotes extensively in his biography. The French capital enchanted the visitor with the grandeur and elegant splendor of its architecture as well as with its wealth of historical monuments presenting visible signs of past greatness. Again and again, he was fascinated by the aesthetic form, yet he missed an emotional content: to him, the French painters were lacking in warmth and inner life, and, therefore, he preferred the Italians such as da Vinci, Perugino, and Raffael. Listening to the accomplished rhetoric of an academic lecture, he saw the rhetorical forms as tricks unworthy of a noble spirit. The reality of Parisian daily life constituted for him a negative contrast to the beauty of art and the majestic past.

He especially disliked Catholicism in which frivolity and piety seemed to mingle freely, in which again form and content seemed to be worlds apart. It is evident that Meyer's Parisian impressions were, to a great extent, determined by his classical-humanistic education and German-Protestant upbringing. As an educated man he reacted foremost to historical monuments, art, and style, and in doing so he experienced, for the first time, the fascination of aesthetic perfection in the external, visible form. Yet as a Protestant and a person who had been immersed in German romanticism he doubted whether such outer beauty could harbor deep, emotional content. To Betsy he expressed this ambivalent feeling in the following way: "...every day I am actually fascinated anew, yet I will find the serious mental nourishment for which I long only in Germany."[27]

When Meyer returned to Zurich at the end of June, 1857, he had acquired a wealth of vivid impressions and a sharper sense for aesthetic effects. But he had not even started his original plan to study law in Paris. Because of Meyer's early return to Zurich Betsy gave up her plans to be trained as a nurse for mental patients. From 1857 on she lived with her brother until he married in 1875. During this period she performed an essential role in Meyer's life: by managing the household she shielded him from the problems of everyday life. But more important was her capability of giving him needed emotional support, because she understood his nature, had a fine sense for literature, and staunchly believed in his talent. In the summer of 1857 Meyer and Betsy spent several weeks in Engelberg in the mountains of central Switzerland. Since the hiking trip with his father in 1838 Meyer had not been in the mountains. He now discovered a landscape and atmosphere congenial to his longings for greatness and purity, longings which had been sharpened, but not satisfied in Paris. The significance of the Alpine landscape is evidenced both in Meyer's life and in his works: almost every summer for three decades he passed some time in the mountains in different parts of Switzerland. The mountains with their majestic contrasts and their virgin silence, removed from the bustle of everyday activity, hold an important place in his work, too: the verse narrative *Engelberg* was inspired by the landscape surrounding this mountain village; the poetry collection contains a cycle entitled "In the Mountains"; and two prose works, *Jürg Jenatsch* and *Die Richterin (The Judge)*, are set in the mountains.

In October of the same year, Meyer made a short trip to Munich.

As in Paris, his interests centered on art and architecture. The variety of the latter was "instructive" to him, but he missed "seriousness and grandeur."[28] Among the painters he liked the Dutch and praised anew Murillo and the Italians for their natural combination of strength and grace; but he passed lightly over the German painters. Germany and Munich did not seem to offer the "serious mental nourishment" which he was seeking; like Paris, Munich left him with an ambivalent impression.

Some months later, in March, 1858, Conrad and Betsy set out on a trip to Italy. They took the most direct route to Rome and stayed there for a little more than two months. This relatively short sojourn in Rome proved to be the most crucial experience for the forming of Meyer's aesthetic concepts and consequently of his poetic world. Unlike Paris and Munich, Rome granted him a total experience in which art and history blended together with the life of the people, in which the aesthetic form established itself naturally as an integral part of the content.

Meyer's interest in the monuments of history — from Roman ruins to Renaissance palaces — was now complemented by a new fascination with the vitality of the people. In the pomp of the Holy Week processions and in the bustle of everyday life Meyer admired the naturally expressive gestures of the Italians. During his second stay in Italy in 1871–1872 he described the fascination which this gesture always had for him in a letter to A. Calmberg: "the Italian gesture is marvellously expressive, almost violent but never abrupt; often close to a grimace and yet never repulsive. One could write an entire chapter about smiling and laughing: they are a true effulgence of the inner life" (*B*, II, 222) The daily contact with such spontaneous and intense emotional expression lent life to Meyer's academic concepts of history and stimulated his imagination. The complement to this discovery of immediacy in daily life was Meyer's experience of the great art treasures of classical antiquity and the Italian Renaissance. Among the many works he admired those of Michelangelo assumed a particular significance for him. Michelangelo's frescoes in the Sistine Chapel and his sculptures contained what Meyer had missed in Paris and Munich, namely, the total fusion of content and form, the complete transformation of inner passion and thought into the form of human beings. This expressiveness struck Meyer all the more because it resulted from concentrating a mass of life experience into a single significant form. Here he was confronted with works which were radically different from his romantic notions of art as characterized by fleeting images, mysterious moods, and lyric forms. In other words: Michelangelo showed him with unmistakable clarity the realistic portrayal of life which Vischer so sorely missed in German art. Although the reading of Vischer's book around 1850 had produced a negative effect on Meyer, the art of Michelangelo now created, years later, the basis on which Vischer's call for realism could come to fruition in Meyer's own way of representing the world.

The results, however, were not visible until much later when Meyer had entered his productive period. He wrote several poems about Michelangelo focusing on the visibility of spiritual elements in his works ("Die Jungfrau," "Il Pensieroso," "In der Sistina") and on the full expression of pain in every gesture ("Michelangelo und seine Statuen"). The bold gestures of many characters in Meyer's novellas are modeled after the compact expression in Michelangelo's sculptures, and — most important — his novellas as well as his poetry are characterized by intense concentration of form and content. This concentration leads, on the one hand, to highly dramatized, often theatrical scenes in the novellas and, on the other hand, to a condensation of symbolic meaning in a single symbol in the lyric poems. Surprisingly, Meyer does not mention Michelangelo in his letters from Rome although he describes a host of other impressions. However, silence about a crucial experience is typical: again and again, Meyer kept his deepest thoughts or feelings hidden until time provided an emotional distance which was the prerequisite for his dealing creatively with such experiences. Thus, the assessment of Michelangelo's impact on Meyer must rest on the Michelangelo poems and on Betsy's memories.

In contrast to his experiences in Paris and Munich, Rome provided Meyer with an unambiguous impression of greatness encompassing past and present, art and life, thoughts and emotions. In this sense, Rome for him came to represent the entire world, leading him to call her, in an early poem, "city of the world" which had forever imparted to him the sense of greatness.[29]

From then on, he admired this greatness, he longed and searched for it in his art, yet he always knew that he himself did not belong to its realm. To his friend and publisher Hermann Haessel he wrote (B, II, 86) "Great style, great art — all my thinking and dreaming lies in this." The word "dreaming" indicates that greatness was a distant ideal for him who was by nature delicate, passive, and reserved. His keen feeling for the discrepancy between his own nature and that of a great, active personality is expressed in the following statement: "The mediocre saddens me because it finds within myself a kindred material — therefore, I am seeking the great with such yearning."[30]

On their way home, Meyer and Betsy stopped in Tuscany. After Rome, Florence appeared small, lacking the cosmopolitan greatness Meyer had sensed "in every corner" in Rome. But their short stay afforded another glimpse of greatness when they visited Baron Bettino Ricasoli who had often been a guest of their mother during his stay in Zurich in 1849. Now Ricasoli was deeply involved in politics, working with enthusiasm and iron will toward the unification of Italy. In him, Meyer met a great man who combined far-reaching visions with decisive action. In the essay about *Huttens Letzte Tage* Meyer stated that Ricasoli's political accomplishments showed him "of what consequence a personality [can be] in the life of a nation."[31] Ricasoli was a living model for Meyer's towering characters who, almost single-handedly, make their mark on the world, for example, Jenatsch, Becket, Gustav Adolf, Pescara.

From Florence the travelers returned to Zurich without further delay. Imbued with the Italian impressions Meyer longed for a quiet life. On May 25, 1858, he wrote to F. von Wyss: "Now that I have seen such greatness and have newly cleared the tablet of my life I gladly return to my books" (*B*, I, 63). In retropect this remark assumes a broader significance in that it sums up the course of Meyer's life: In 1857–1858 he went out to encounter the world, gathering a host of basic, lasting images; then he returned to Zurich and became absorbed in digesting and transforming his experiences. Between 1859 and 1891 he only took three other trips which led him beyond the Swiss borders: he spent the winter of 1871–1872 in Verona and Venice; he spent his honeymoon in 1875 on the island of Corsica; and, in 1880, he made a very short excursion to Leipzig, Dresden, and Berlin. Although the Venetian impressions enlarged Meyer's view of Italy they were similar to those received in Rome. About the trip to Germany very little is known, since Meyer passed it over in silence. Thus, the three journeys to Paris, Munich, and Rome constitute Meyer's only direct contact with the world outside Switzerland, the world of great history and art which were to play such an important role in his work.

III *Slow development and rich harvest (1859–1898)*

For all its essential experiences the Italian journey did not cause any immediate change in Meyer's life. In Zurich he resumed his translator's work, translating now from German into French. But only the translation of the mostly factual, explanatory texts for the luxury edition of Jakob Ulrich's *Die Schweiz in Bildern (Switzerland in Images)* was published. He did not find a publisher for his *Jeanne de Naples*, a translation of Platen's *Geschichten des Königreiches Neapel (Stories of the Kingdom of Naples)*. A short story, *Clara*, that he appears to have written in 1854–1855, remained for years his only tangible attempt at creative writing; it was not published until 1938. In his spare time Meyer associated with a few friends such as Rochat, the legal historian Friedrich von Wyss, and Mathilde Escher, a woman of exceptional practical talents which she devoted entirely to creating and heading benevolent societies. She took a motherly interest in Betsy and Conrad, whom she would have liked to see married so that he would become more independent from his sister and more securly settled.

Meyer's early relationships with women were complicated because his reserved nature and his lack of a secure position made him behave timidly toward them. In addition, he often deluded himself by mistaking friendliness for love. This is already evident in his behavior toward two women he knew in Lausanne in 1853: having no profession, he did not dare continue his social contacts with Alexandrine Marquis. He then conceived a romantic plan to marry Constance von Rodt; he would wait for three years when she would be seventeen and he would have a position. This shows that Meyer longed for marriage while fearing its responsibilities. In Zurich, between 1857 and 1860 he formed attachments to three women: Maria Burckhardt, Pauline Escher, and Clelia Weydmann. These attachments existed mainly in his imagination, but when faced with reality he was so deeply hurt that he fled Zurich twice — after the disappointment with Maria in 1858 he hurried off to Rome, and after that with Clelia in 1860 he returned to Lausanne again. In the case of Pauline Escher we possess a letter from Meyer to her, dated March 25, 1859.[32] This letter is revealing in two respects: the fact that Meyer proposed to Pauline through a mutual friend indicates both his timidity and a scrupulous adherence to social form; and the reserved, even formal tone of the letter lends proof to the assumption that Meyer's relationship with Pauline as well as with other women lacked intimacy. On the whole, we have little direct information concerning Meyer's love episodes. An account of this aspect of his life can be found in Lena F. Dahme's

Women in the Life and the Art of Conrad Ferdinand Meyer.[33] Despite a meticulous collection of all the scattered remarks by Meyer himself and of reports by others these episodes remain vague. Lena Dahme also often overshoots the mark by establishing too many direct connections between these episodes and Meyer's works.[34]

As already mentioned, Meyer went to Lausanne again, where he spent most of the year 1860. Zurich had become intolerable for him because his misfortune with women aggravated his feeling of inferiority for not having a regular profession. Determined to remedy this situation he wanted to engage in literary studies which would enable him to become a professor of French literature in a German-speaking country. But since he had neither proper professional guidance nor training his studies lacked planning and coherence. First, he concentrated on the Epistles of Paul in the original Greek, then on Goethe's correspondence with the famous Zurich physiognomist Johann Caspar Lavater. Despite Meyer's good intentions these projects were soon superseded by a more absorbing activity, namely writing new and revising old poems. In November, 1860, he was ready to submit a collection of one hundred poems entitled *Bilder und Balladen von Ulrich Meister* (*Images and Ballads by Ulrich Meister*) to the publisher J. J. Weber in Leipzig. Weber declared that he was unable to print the book, which he nevertheless called valuable, and Meyer did not follow his advice to send the book to other publishers. Insignificant as this episode may appear, it is important for Meyer's development. For the first time, he put his poetic work together and subjected it to an outside opinion. Even more remarkable, Weber's rejection did not deter him from continuing to write. His decision to become a poet was now more firm and was accompanied by a new awareness of his need to elicit constructive criticism in order to learn. He was, however, too timid to approach anybody in Zurich's literary circles, least of all Gottfried Keller, who had already made a name for himself as an author of poetry and prose. Thus, Meyer resorted to an old friend from Neuchâtel, Félix Bovet, a librarian and theology professor. Although Bovet was but little qualified to act as Meyer's poetic mentor, he finally consented. Even if his praise was often too generous and his criticism not very precise he performed an essential role by strengthening Meyer's confidence and stimulating him to rework his poems.

Extensive and careful rewriting was from then on the characteristic element of Meyer's working method and the vehicle of his poetic development. Bovet's role as critic lasted only for a short time, and Meyer was soon left to himself. In 1863, he received some criticism from Gustav Pfizer's wife. Betsy had shown her brother's poems to Mrs. Pfizer in the hope that she or her husband could help to find a publisher. But it was Betsy who persuaded Metzler in Stuttgart to print the poems at Meyer's own expense; for their printing Meyer thoroughly revised the poems, which were then published in 1864 under the title *Zwanzig Balladen von einem Schweizer (Twenty Ballads written by a Swiss).* Compared with the poems of 1860 these ballads show progress toward a more compact narration and a more vigorous expression, but Meyer had not yet overcome his tendency to verbose, overdetailed descriptions, nor had he found a truly individual style. However, the small volume already contains a stock of themes fundamental to his poetic world, such as the dramatic juxtaposition of young life and sudden death, past glory and present dejection, crime and conscience, convent and worldly life. All but two of these ballads were later reworked and incorporated into the poetry collection of 1882; for example, "Die Stadt am Meer" ("City on the Sea," later "Venedigs erster Tag" — "Venice's First Day"), "Der Mönch von Bonifacio" ("The Monk of Bonifacio"), "Don Juan de Austria" (later "Das Auge des Blinden" — "The Eye of the Blind"), "Die Römerin" ("The Roman Woman," later "Der Gesang der Parze" — "Song of a Parca"), "Thespesius," "Der Hugenott" ("The Huguenot," later "Die Füsse im Feuer" — "Feet in the Fire").

Understandably, the slender volume found but little echo in the literary world. There were only two reviews — one written by Vulliemin in the *Bibliothèque Universelle,* another in the magazine *Die Schweiz.* In Zurich, however, the book meant a personal success for Meyer: at the age of thirty-nine he finally could show an accomplishment. The manuscripts of the following years attest to a growing productivity as well as to a constant reworking of old poems. New possibilities also arose: in 1865, the *Stuttgarter Morgenblatt* agreed, on Pfizer's recommendation, to publish a number of poems, and others were published in the Swiss periodical *Die Alpenrosen* in 1866 and 1867. How firm Meyer's commitment to writing now was is evidenced by his refusing two less creative projects: a translation of lectures by the Geneva philosopher Ernest Naville[35] and the compilation of an anthology. The latter was proposed to him by the Leipzig publisher Hermann Haessel, whom Meyer had met in connection with the Naville translation. This casual acquaintance soon developed into a friendly relation between author and publisher: Haessel printed all of Meyer's works in book form.

Meyer and Betsy also were introduced to François and Eliza Wille and became regular guests at their house "Mariafeld," which was a meeting place for writers, artists, and scholars. Here Meyer met Wagner's friend Mathilde Wesendonck, the architect Gottfried Semper, the German writers Gottfried Kinkel and Adolf Calmberg — both living in Zurich — and once he met Gottfried Keller, who was but a rare guest at such fashionable intellectual gatherings. Thus, Meyer received the benefit of broad literary discussions. Wille (1811–1896) soon sensed Meyer's talent and afforded him active encouragement and patronage. For this Meyer was deeply grateful, although Wille's strong personality and his often dogmatic attitudes were sometimes problematic, if not offensive, to Meyer's reserved nature. Yet Meyer also admired the strength and worldly experience of Wille, who had led a rather turbulent life (together with the young Bismarck) as a student in Germany and as a political journalist.

The period of the late 1860s brings a broadening of Meyer's everyday life. Through the Wille circle he was in direct, though loose, contact with the world of German literature. In the external form of his life there was a change, too: in 1868, Meyer and Betsy moved out of Zurich to Küsnacht, where they lived right on the lake. From then on, Meyer always chose to live outside the city and near the lake — in Meilen (1872–1875), in Küsnacht (1876–1877), and in Kilchberg (1877 to his death in 1898). The lake, which had been a comforting place in his solitary years, was now part of his immediate environment; in his work, especially in the poetry, the lake is one of the central symbols. It was also in this period that Meyer ventured into his first larger work, a historical novella or novel about Georg Jenatsch, who had played a controversial, if not heroic role in the political world of Graubünden during the Thirty Years War. But the material proved so vast and complex that he turned to other projects before finishing *Jürg Jenatsch* in 1873–1874, after a long maturing process. A new volume of poetry — *Romanzen und Bilder (Ballads and Images)* — appeared for Christmas 1869 (predated 1870), the first book bearing Meyer's name. The poems are divided into two parts: "Stimmung" (Mood) contains thirty-three lyric poems while "Erzählung" (Narrative) includes twenty-one ballads. This book is marked by a much more personal style in the lyric images as well as in the language, and many lyric poems already show the stylistic condensation which was to become a hallmark of Meyer's art. However, the volume went almost unnoticed except for one positive review in a German literary magazine. The Swiss critics remained silent — Meyer was still unknown.

This changed significantly when, in the fall of 1871, his verse narrative *Huttens letzte Tage (Hutten's Last Days)* was published. The critics in Switzerland reacted quickly and very positively, and growing praise from Germany followed. Almost overnight Meyer passed from obsurity to fame. The reason for this success was twofold. First, it lay in the artistic accomplishment, the work's unity of form and content. But, second, the success was conditioned even more by the historical events of that time. Ulrich von Hutten (1488–1523), who fought not only for the Reformation but for a unified and strong Germany, was considered a national hero since the mid-eighteenth century. In recapturing the dramatic events of his life as well as his early and solitary death in exile Meyer struck a most responsive chord in a public that overwhelmingly acclaimed Bismarck's politics and the founding of a German Empire under the domination of Prussia.

Most critics took and take Meyer at his word in his essay of 1891 "Mein Erstling *Huttens letzte Tage*" ("My First Work *Hutten's Last Days*") in which he pictures himself as a fervent partisan of Prussian domination. In the same vein, Meyer told Anton Reitler in 1885: "1870 was a critical year for me. The great war ... also decided a war in my soul. Deeply stirred by a feeling of identity with the Germans, a feeling that had imperceptibly matured, I discarded my French nature at this moment of world-historical significance, and I wrote *Hutten* under an inner compulsion to express this change of mind."[36] But such a complete about-face seems unlikely when we consider Meyer's deep attachment to his friends in the French part of Switzerland and to everything they represented — French culture as well as his personal liberation in 1852–1853. In an elucidating article, David A. Jackson gives a much more convincing assessment of Meyer's position at that time.[37] Focusing on remarks that have seldom been quoted in this context Jackson shows that Meyer had misgivings about the ruthless and violent aspects of German politics. Yet he also realized that he depended for his own literary success on the patronage of the

Wille circle, where Bismarck and Prussia were enthusiastically supported. In a letter to the historian Georg von Wyss, Meyer describes his dilemma: "For me, too, it was difficult to overcome my French sympathies; but a decision had in God's name to be made since the French-German conflict will probably dominate decades and will make any middle position in literary matters untenable" (*B*, I. 33). Meyer's decision, however, was not a clear-cut partisanship for Germany but a compromise, a decision to go along with the times without completely sacrificing his own more liberal ideas.

This situation is reminiscent of the one in Préfargier in 1852–1853 when, in order to preserve his plan of a writing career, he had to profess to have renounced this very plan. Both the situation and the reaction are typical for Meyer: his unusual development forced him into positions of dependence, but since he was not rebellious by nature he chose a conditional compliance that would satisfy the requirements of the outside world and still give him some freedom to express his innermost thoughts. During Meyer's creative period this situation remained basically the same: he never felt completely in step with the general attitudes of his time, yet still needed approval from his contemporaries. Therefore, one must be very careful in interpreting his statements, especially if they are aimed at a larger public. By the same token, his works have to be analyzed with the fact in mind that he has a double message to convey — an obvious one for the general public representing the general attitudes of the times, and a more secret and personal one that corresponds more closely to the deeper complexities of his time.

Hutten was a milestone in Meyer's life, marking the end of his painfully slow development and the start of two decades of productivity. This breakthrough to successful and uninterrupted creative writing is all the more surprising when we consider Meyer's age: he was forty-six in 1871 and sixty-six when he completed his last novella, *Angela Borgia,* in 1891. The biographical account of these twenty years can be relatively short, since the course of Meyer's external life became more and more stable while his internal life was absorbed in his writing; it can thus be discussed as it finds reflection in his works.

With Betsy, Meyer spent the winter of 1871–1872 in Verona and Venice. Despite a good deal of sightseeing, his main occupation was writing. He completed the first version of the verse narrative *Engelberg* and also worked on those parts of *Jenatsch* which take place in

Venice. After returning to Switzerland Meyer and his sister resumed their quiet life in a new home in Meilen. In 1875, however a major change occurred when Meyer married Luise Ziegler (1837–1915), whom he had known for several years. Since they were both rather advanced in age, their union probably was prompted less by passion than by a feeling of companionship which Meyer expressed in a poem to Luise with the following words:

> Ich weiss von Zwei 'n,
> Die beiden haben
> Ein jedes still für sich allein
> Des Herzens Schatz vergraben.

> So häuften sie
> Ein ungelebtes Leben. . . .[38]

> I know of two,
> Both of them have
> each for himself
> buried the heart's treasure.

> Thus, they have stored
> An unlived life. . . .

For Meyer, another element was of prime importance although it remained unexpressed. Luise belonged to one of Zurich's oldest and most respected patrician families, and by marrying her Meyer regained a place in the society which had rejected him in his youth and which was little inclined to readmit him solely on the basis of literary achievement. Unable to be a revolutionary and to turn his back on this unsympathetic world he longed to be fully reaccepted in Zurich's upper class. This social recognition was for him a vital complement to his literary success. It is in this larger context that his marriage to Luise Ziegler must be assessed. As a typical representative of Zurich's old families with their tradition of business, military, and political careers she was realistic and efficient. She also shared Meyer's reserved nature. For literature and art in general she had but a limited understanding, although she had received some instruction in landscape painting. Paintings made during her marriage show a rather mediocre technique and little individual expression.[39] However, if she did not — and could not — share

Meyer's creative work, she could give him what he needed at this point: a firm rooting in the normal life of the bourgeoisie with social contacts and obligations and the security of larger financial means. This bourgeois existence counterbalanced Meyer's inner life with its dark depths and dizzying contrasts. The wedding on October 5, 1875, was followed by a trip to Lausanne, southern France, and the island of Corsica which the couple liked so much that they extended their stay by two months until January, 1876. Once again, Meyer was enraptured with the colors and the intensity of life in the South; reflections of this experience can be found in the poems "Abschied von Korsika" ("Farewell to Corsica") and "Weihnacht in Ajaccio" ("Christmas in Ajaccio").

After the return to Küsnacht, Meyer's life took on a form quite different from that of the late 1860s and early 1870s when his attention was centered exclusively on his writings and contacts with other artists in the Wille circle. Now he was part of Zurich's high society and had to fulfill numerous social obligations which, according to his letters, occupied his free time to a considerable extent. In 1877, the couple bought a house in Kilchberg, a small town located on a hill with an enchanting view of Zurich, the entire lake and the Alps in the distance. To Haessel he wrote on February 17, 1877: "The house is spacious but old. The view is indeed the most beautiful on the lake of Zurich. A large orchard, for the first time my very own private soil, may favor my muse" (*B*, II, 68). Two years later, in 1879, a daughter — Camilla Elisabeth — was born. Thus, Meyer's life was complete with the duties of a family man and home owner. The very limitations of this bourgeois existence provided him with the hold on reality which he needed in this period of ceaseless productivity. This is expressed in a letter to Hermann Lingg: "My wife with her Spartan habits and with her very natural behavior is truly beneficent to me, and my five-year-old little child amuses me without worrying me yet. I myself am gray and sometimes have rheumatism, but I possess an inner unmotivated, original serenity...."[40] Between 1876 and 1887 Meyer was able to publish a new work almost every year. Writing these works demanded not only hard and intense work every day from about 9:00 A.M. to 2:00 P.M., but also put a great strain on his inner life, because in this internal realm he was, as the analysis of his work will show, forced again and again to probe into the established values on which rested his existence within bourgeois society.

Meyer's marriage also brought a change in his relationship with

Betsy, who had shared his daily life as well as his creative work. Although Betsy acted as her brother's secretary until 1879, she was determined to withdraw from this close association with him in order to avoid antagonizing Luise who was exluded from this literary realm. The developments in 1891 proved her fear to be justified. Thus, Betsy did not accept the invitation to live with her brother and his wife in Kilchberg, but led a life of her own. In 1880, she found an opportunity to realize her old project of taking care of emotionally disturbed people by associating herself with a small private institution which was based on Christian charity and the belief in prayer healing.[41] In her stead, a younger relative, Fritz Meyer, took over the job of secretary until 1889.

Between 1876 and 1887 Meyer felt more comfortable than ever before. He had a socially respected position in Zurich, and his literary production earned him a widening recognition in Germany. The latter is mirrored in his correspondence with German writers — with the well-known Paul Heyse, with Hermann Lingg, and with Luise von François, a distinguished author of historical novels. Julius Rodenberg, the editor of the highly respected literary journal *Deutsche Rundschau,* invited Meyer to publish his works in this periodical in which the new prose of such leading authors as Gottfried Keller, Theodor Storm, and Paul Heyse appeared. Starting with *Der Heilige* in 1879 Meyer then published all but one of his novellas in the *Deutsche Rundschau* before Haessel printed them — once more revised — as books, and Meyer was now on a friendly, though distant footing with Gottfried Keller, his famous compatriot who, twenty years earlier, had seemed out of reach to the then would-be writer; despite essential differences in attitude and style Keller and Meyer valued each other's works. In 1880, the University of Zurich awarded Meyer an honorary doctoral degree. How much this official recognition — one which his father had also received — meant to him can be seen in the fact that he used this title on his cards and at times even in his signature. A German decoration came in 1888 when he received the Bavarian order of Maximilian. As a local celebrity and a part of Zurich's cultural life he wrote poems for such occasions as the opening of a Swiss National Exhibit (1883), the dedication of a statue for the Zurich reformer Huldrych Zwingli (1885), and the inauguration of a new theater (1891).

Among young writers seeking counsel from such a recognized master was the Swiss Carl Spitteler (1845–1924) who impressed

Meyer as "an indisputably rare talent" worthy of support. In his house Meyer received many visitors from Germany: there were his correspondents Haessel, Rodenberg, and Luise von François; others wanted to meet him because they were writing about him (Hermann Friedrichs in 1881; Anton Reitler in 1885; and Fritz Kögel in 1890). In 1877, Meyer also became acquainted with Adolf Frey, a young Swiss poet and literary historian who subsequently reviewed several of Meyer's works. Since Meyer liked this young friend and his critical work he designated him as his biographer; the first edition of Frey's biography appeared in 1900, and a third, definitively revised one in 1919. Despite its limitations, this book remains essential for everyone studying Meyer's life and work. With his growing reputation at home and abroad, Meyer continued to lead a solitary life. The Zurich public often misjudged his works, and despite his contacts with German men of letters he had no desire to become involved in the literary life of Germany; even on his short trip to Leipzig, Dresden, and Berlin in 1880 he failed to seek literary German company. Comments in his letters about his readings, however, show that he was interested in the new contemporary literature — Ibsen, Hauptmann, Turgenev, Tolstoi, and Dostoevski. But the brevity of his comments indicates that Meyer had little inclination for a theoretical consideration of literature. Therefore, his reviews are few in number and limited in critical perception. In his own writing, however, Meyer gives living proof of a superior critical sense in slowly turning a mediocre poem into a unique work of art.

An often laconic brevity is also typical for Meyer's letters which, after 1875, are mostly filled with tedious details of his daily obligations. His epistolary style seems designed to hide rather than disclose his actual thoughts and feelings. A seeming contrast to this was his conversation. According to his visitors, he talked in a lively manner about his past and present works as well as his plans. Thus, he appeared as an inspired writer mastering a vast empire of contrasting figures and forces. Both attitudes are true expressions of his character, and neither one can be claimed as showing his entire, real personality. Their discrepancy stems from the fact that both are reactions to Meyer's experiences of life's darkness and basic uncertainty. He needed both — the shelter of an ordered existence as a respected citizen and the escape into the world of great action. Thus, it comes as no surprise that his statements about his writings can be contradictory and have to be carefully considered within a larger context. The same is true for the biographical details of his life: they create the image of a contradictory and elusive personality: there is the "saint of Kilchberg," as Heyse once put it, an ascetic priest of high art, and the epicurean, enjoying his comfortable life of which his growing corpulence was a visible sign; there is a religious skeptic in his work, yet a Christian *pater familias* who read a Bible passage every day to the entire household. These details can be integrated only when related to Meyer's personality in his time, that is to say, to the complicated reactions of a complex character in a period of rapid changes.

At the end of 1887, Meyer's creative period was interrupted. For almost a year he was incapacitated by rheumatic fevers and nervous disorders as well as depressions. In 1889 he started again on old plans, namely, on a drama about the Hohenstaufen Emperor Frederick II and a large novel dealing with the count of Toggenburg, a sort of Renaissance potentate in fifteenth-century Switzerland. Late in 1889 he engaged in yet another project, *Angela Borgia,* which soon absorbed him completely. The completion of the work in the summer of 1891 turned into a painful tour de force since Rodenberg's deadline seemed to assume for Meyer the meaning of an ultimate test of his productivity. Once again, Betsy had to act as secretary, not only because Fritz Meyer was no longer available but because Meyer needed her support for the final revision of this work, which he once called his "most difficult" task. In this time of intense effort the hidden conflict between Betsy and Luise was aggravated. These problems were deeply rooted in their different attitude toward Meyer's work: for Betsy, it had absolute priority while, for Luise, it now became more and more a threat to her and her husband's well-being. Luise could not understand the writer's plight, his desperate need to finish, to realize himself once more in the face of age, sickness, and death. Therefore, she tried to protect him from his work and viewed Betsy, the faithful collaborator, as a harmful influence.

The completion of *Angela Borgia* failed to alleviate the strain on Meyer's nerves. At first, he tried to convince others and himself that he was seriously working on his cherished plans. But signs of physical and psychological overexertion accumulated and made real work even less possible. In 1892, he was plagued by delusions and, with his approval, he was transferred to the Institution of Königsfelden in July, 1892, forty years after his entrance in Préfargier. According to the psychological study of A. Kielholz,[42]

Meyer's condition in 1892 resembled that of 1852 in that he again believed he repelled everybody by emanating a bad odor. For a while he regressed to the state of an infant who had to be fed and cleaned. Kielholz interprets this and some of his fantasies as fulfillments of wishes that reality had never fulfilled — for example, he fused the images of his sister and his wife into one, and he addressed a visiting friend as king and a patient as Bismarck. At the same time, he was tortured by fantasies of financial ruin, of being sentenced and executed, of being persecuted by wild animals. While a specific definition of Meyer's illness is difficult, it can be said that in 1892 he suffered an acute psychosis which subsided to a chronic state so that in September, 1893 he could return to Kilchberg.

He had recovered to the point where he could lead a relatively normal, though withdrawn life, knowing again who he was and in which century he lived. Under the care of his wife he even took shorter trips to the Lake of Geneva, to Strassburg, and to the Alps. Yet his spirit was broken and he lost all real contact with his former life and his work. Being completely dependent on his wife with her aversion to his writing and her rather narrow Christian ideas, he viewed his biographer Adolf Frey as a deadly persecutor and his sister Betsy as the misfortune of his life, while attributing all the happiness he had ever experienced to Luise. According to Hans-Günther Bressler[43] these projections of his problems onto other people might have furthered a certain normalcy in his behavior. At times he even wrote poems: they are mostly of a religious content and are couched in colorless language — a far cry from his earlier poetry with its shaded nuances and forceful concentration. The following stanzas of a seven-stanza poem "Stern und Glauben" ("Stars and Faith") shall serve as an example that offers a startling contrast to other poems with the same star motif, for example, "Schwüle" ("Sultry Day") and "Unter Sternen" ("Under the Stars"):

> Stern füllen über mir den dunklen Raum,
> Und mir wird die ganze Welt zum Traum.
> Sterne, sagt, was redet ihr mir zu?
> Seid ihr stumm? Sprecht laut, ich lausche hier.
>
> Redet! Für die andern Wesen seid ihr stumm.
> Flüstert nur, ich hör' es rings herum.
> Mären hör' ich lieblich, redet ihr,
> Ich vernehme eure Stimme hier.

Was ihr sagt, ich hör es alles gern,
Ihr erzählet mir von Gott dem Herrn. [44]

Stars fill the dark space above me,
And the whole world becomes a dream for me.
Stars, tell, what are you saying to me?
Are you mute? Speak loudly, I am listening here.

Speak! for other beings you are mute.
Whisper only, I can hear it all around.
Lovely fairy tales, I hear, you tell,
I perceive your voices here.
What you say, I like to hear it all,
You are telling me about God the Lord.

As Alfred Zäch points out, Luise used to copy the poems and showed them to influential friends, hoping that they might prove Meyer's health and reawakened creativity. However, she also admitted that Meyer would not have consented to publishing them because he was convinced that all he did now was worthless. Despite his intellectual debilitation he apparently had preserved a critical sense.

In the fall of 1898, his condition seemed to improve, and he was, according to Luise's report, as lively as in former days and had no difficulties answering all of Camilla's questions about literature and history. But this was a last flaring up of his life: on November 28, 1898, while reading the *Deutsche Rundschau,* which had spread his name throughout Germany, he died suddenly of a stroke.

CHAPTER 2

History — World Seen at a Distance

HISTORY is present almost everywhere in Meyer's writings. All his longer works — except *Engelberg* — have either historical characters as protagonists or a historical background for an invented story, and the poetry collection includes a large number of historical ballads. Such a consistent preference for historical material as a means of poetic expression must be significant for Meyer's writing in general, that is to say, for his basic attitudes toward the world and toward art.

In his early childhood Meyer was introduced to the realm of history by his father who, as a passionate historian, entertained his children with real stories about historical events. As Betsy tells us,[1] his vivid narration filled her and her brother's imagination with scenes of Greeks and Romans, Charlemagne and the German emperors. With his strong historical interests Meyer's father was a representative of the contemporary interest in history — one which led to an unprecedented rise of historical studies and which gained the nineteenth century the title "the century of history." This trend was reflected on many levels, for instance, in the historical ballads that filled Meyer's reader in the gymnasium as well as in the nationalistic orientation that began to surface in the European countries. While these external influences were important in rousing and fostering Meyer's historical interest, only their combining with aspects of the writer's personality could cause such an almost exclusive predilection for history as his working material. Starting with his father's stories about ancient Rome and medieval Germany and all through his own readings and experiences of the past in Paris and Rome, history became the realm of great individuals and their heroic deeds, of power and passion, of momentous decisions affecting a large world. In other words, history was a realm

45

contrary to Meyer's own life with all its confining elements. Thus, it is no wonder that Meyer was fascinated with historical figures who had power over a large or small world, for example, Charlemagne and Stemma the Judge, King Henry II of England and the Italian city tyrant Ezzelino da Romano. He was even more absorbed by men such as Thomas Becket, who overcame great odds and acquired the power to set a stamp on the world.

Characterized by greatness and action, this historical world is built on Meyer's personal longings; it is a *Sehnsuchtswelt*. But at the same time, this world represents a much larger phenomenon, namely, the longing of the educated bourgeois of the second half of the nineteenth century for a world dominated by great individuals and powerful ideas and not by amorphous masses and tedious political wrangling. The feeling of living in an insignificant time furthered the interest in the past. This attitude manifests itself simultaneously in the works of many authors, most prominently in Wagner's operas with their glorification of legendary German heroes, and in Nietzsche's scathing attacks on contemporary mediocrity and the lack of forceful leadership. Meyer's and Nietzsche's views of the Dionysian element and of the Italian Renaissance bear a strong resemblance, which is striking both because Meyer apparently did not hear anything about Nietzsche until around 1884[2] when his concepts had long been formed, and because he is known to have read only one book by Nietzsche — *Beyond Good and Evil* — around 1887–1888. This resemblance of ideas without direct influence adds further proof to the fact that Meyer's love for great history transcends his personal longings and expresses a general attitude of the time. And this accounts in good part for the success of Meyer's prose works dealing with history.

But history is more than just a compensatory, ideal world which would actually shut out Meyer's most personal experiences in the dark years between 1840 and 1857. Although he later passed over this period in virtual silence, it significantly affected his view of history, of the world, and of life. At that time his refusal to conform to a promising bourgeois role made him insecure regarding himself and his environment. He questioned the value of the established social and religious codes, but Pfizer's judgment of his poems and his own reading of Vischer, in turn, questioned his own set of aesthetic values, thus leaving him in the void. This harrowing experience generated both a basic doubt of any established value and a craving for fixed ideal values with the reassurance they offered. All this was so essential that Meyer had to find a way of expressing it without having to expose his innermost suffering. He voiced this need much later in a letter to Bovet of June 24, 1877: "It is less the craft itself which tempts me [to write] . . . than *certain depths of the soul* to which I would like to descend in no matter what form"(*B*,I, 129). History offered him a suitable form with its factual yet puzzling material which allows, even asks, for an interpretation probing into the depths of complex psychological motivations. By selecting enigmatic historical figures as protagonists and turbulent periods as background for his work, Meyer was able to convert his subjective experiences into a more objective material, the very one that represented the values of his *Sehnsuchtswelt.*

Thus, history becomes a mask. On the surface, it embodies political power, success, heroic sacrifice, staunch religious belief, unconditional love. But at the same time, history incorporates Meyer's doubts concerning these ideal values and prompts him to view events and characters in an ambivalent light. He achieves this by setting off the ideal values against dubious aspects: Jenatsch's ardent patriotism is accompanied by boundless greed for power, Becket's saintliness could originate in a most subtle scheme of personal vengeance, Schadau's staunch defense of protestantism in *Das Amulett (The Amulet)* has adverse results, and Astorre's and Antiope's fervid love promotes chaos in *Die Hochzeit des Mönchs (The Monk's Wedding).* The double nature of history is also expressed in another letter to Bovet of December 14, 1888: "I am using the form of the historical novella solely in order to lodge in it my experiences and my personal feelings, preferring it to the novel dealing with the present [*Zeitroman*] because it masks me better and places the reader at a greater distance. Thus, with a very objective and eminently artistic form I am internally fully individual and subjective" (*B*, I, 138). Using history as a mask provides the objectifying distance Meyer needs if he is to voice his deepest and most disquieting experiences and thoughts.

This last quotation further elucidates the dimensions of such a distancing mask. By setting his personal doubts back into a remote and objective past the temporal distance becomes a protective shield against them. In a letter of May 19, 1887 to L. von François he therefore calls the present "too crude and too close for me." The author's inner distance also entails a distance toward the reader; Meyer does not want him fully to identify with the story, but rather to be a detached, attentive spectator. Such an attitude on the part of the reader corresponds to an ironic stance from which Meyer indirectly criticizes his own time by exposing errors of the past. To François, he wrote in May, 1881: "I like best to steep myself in bygone days whose errors (and with them the erring generally inherent in man) I treat with subtle irony. [Using the past] also allows me to treat the eternally human in a more artistic manner than the brutal immediacy of contemporary material would permit." Again, as in the above quoted letter to Bovet, Meyer stresses the fact that distance — here in the form of irony — is for him a crucial element not only of history but also of art.

At this point, Meyer's concept of art has to be brought into focus. The preceding explanations about the function of distance show that his writing cannot be judged by the principle of immediacy in subjective expression. In Meyer's time this latter principle was still prevalent as a consequence of classical-romantic literature whose value was in part gauged by its subjectivity, its direct, personal expression. As admirer of this literature Meyer first tried to imitate it, but his reading of Vischer and his encounter with Italian art[3] opened a new stylistic possibility to him: he came to recognize the importance of objective, visual images. By reworking his poems over and over again, by experimenting with *Jenatsch, Hutten,* and *Engelberg,* he gropingly develops his own style which corresponds to his need for distance: he aims at objective images with carefully wrought effects, at mere descriptions which subtly reveal subjective feelings and thoughts as well as the author's personal symbolism. The inner world of the characters is transposed into external images so as to avoid abstract depictions or directly subjective comments. Betsy records Meyer as summarizing his concept of art in the following way: "In creative writing [*Poesie*] every thought has to move as a visible shape. No reasoning, no abstract description must be left unintegrated. Everything must be movement and beauty."[4]

With such importance placed on visible movement the effective groupings and lightings of each scene are emphasized; the formal, aesthetic element prevails as characteristic of Meyer's art. Whether or not this entails a neglect of the ethical content will be discussed later in connection with individual works. Of special interest here is the fact that the pictorial nature of Meyer's writings again implies distance on the part of both writer and reader. Events and characters are captured in a series of scenes, even dramatic tableaux forming compact and, therefore, rather distant entities which do not offer the reader an opportunity to feel included, to find — so to speak — a way leading into the picture. In many cases, this exclusion is obvious when a scene is presented within a frame separating the reader/viewer from the scene itself. Often such frames are provided by open doors and windows, and at times even by real paintings whose descriptions constitute essential elements of a story — for example, the huge painting through which the unfathomable nature of Pescara is first introduced.

On the larger scale of narrative form Meyer creates distance by using a narrator whose reasons for remembering and telling a specific story provide an often contrasting frame for the story itself. And since he chooses persons of the past as narrating past events the stories are twice removed from the reader. The importance of this distancing device is born out by the fact that Meyer used it in five of his eleven prose works. He also refines the basic form by combining the story proper with a series of interruptions that force the reader to pause and contemplate. This attests also to the writer's own need for detachment. Meyer summarized the function of this complex form in a letter to the writer Paul Heyse of November 12, 1884: "With me, the inclination for frames is quite instinctive. I like to keep a subject at distance or, better, to keep it as far as possible from my eyes, and then it seems to me [that] the indirect way of narrating (and the interruptions, too) mitigate the harshness of the story" (*B*, II, 340–41). Like the historical material itself the framed form serves as protection for the vulnerable author.

Meyer's vital need for distance is thus expressed in both content (history) and form (irony, framework). Therefore, he does not fit the image of the writer in the classical-romantic tradition in which inspiration, immediate expression, and direct addressing of the reader are key elements. Meyer's creativity functions in a quite different way since, for him, impression and creative expression are separated. Direct impressions — however strong they may be — do not impel him to express them immediately; instead, they are carefully registered but not used until, considerably later, they combine with the impulses gathered mainly from books, historical studies, and art works. As the development of many poems shows, inspiration, for Meyer, may come either late, that is after he has already worked for quite a while on an idea, or in piecemeal at different stages of a lengthy process that slowly transforms a rather mediocre initial idea into a poem of rare beauty. Again, temporal distance is an essential factor that allows Meyer to deal creatively with his inner life, which Heinrich Henel accurately calls a "'idden treasure."[5] If direct emotional impact is, for many poets, the main source of inspiration it is more of a deterrent for Meyer.

He finds creative impulses again and again in that which is already shaped — in paintings and sculptures, in mythological figures, historical characters, and events. With preshaped forms and cultural knowledge providing molds for his thoughts, it is obvious that his creative accomplishment does not lie primarily in inventing stories; instead, it lies in his very choice and combination of such material and in his ability to unfold in it a new, uniquely symbolic significance. There is no doubt that he depends on classical knowledge, that he is a *Bildungsdichter,* but with this knowledge he creates a world which is unmistakably his own in form and meaning.

Meyer's historical works fall into two basic types. First, there are those in which historical characters and events make up the main part of the plot: *Huttens letzte Tage (Hutten's Last Days), Jürg Jenatsch, Der Heilige (The Saint), Gustav Adolfs Page (Gustav Adolf's Page), Die Versuchung des Pescara (The Temptation of Pescara),* and *Angela Borgia.* In a second group are those in which the main characters and action are invented but are given a specific historical background: *Das Amulett (The Amulet), Der Schuss von der Kanzel (The Shot from the Pulpit), Das Leiden eines Knaben (The Sufferings of a Boy), Plautus im Nonnenkloster (Plautus in the Nunnery), Die Hochzeit des Mönchs (The Monk's Wedding),* and *Die Richterin (The Judge).* Different kinds of sources play an important role. Alfred Zäch's excellent commentaries on Meyer's prose works and verse narratives list, in the historical-critical edition, the sources Meyer is known to have used as well as those he might have used; impulses received from a variety of literary and art works are pointed out, too. Thus, it is shown in how many instances Meyer was inspired by the work of others. In a separate edition of *Die Versuchung des Pescara,* Gustav Beckers presents the most exhaustive of such studies in which he meticulously traces any possible congruences, even in the use of words, between Meyer's text and the historical sources.[6] Yet this close adherence to historical facts is counterbalanced by significant deviations. Even in the works with historical protagonists Meyer does not shy away from adding unhistorical characters, events or relationships — for example, his Thomas Becket has a daughter who is seduced by King Henry, and Gustav Adolf is accompanied by a girl disguised as his page. Such changes are designed to shed new light on historical events and to enlarge the realm of psychological motivation. In every work, all the adopted details are integrated in Meyer's own vision of history, of the world seen at a distance but filled with his personal insights.

CHAPTER 3

The Importance of Form

I   Huttens letzte Tage

THOUGH the verse cycle *Huttens letzte Tage* (*Hutten's Last Days,* 1871) was Meyer's third publication and the second bearing his name the author used to call it "his first work" (*Erstling*). This designation is, of course, justified by the fact that with *Hutten* the hitherto unknown author successfully broke into the German-speaking literary world. Yet there is another, internal justification: in this work Meyer realized for the first time his poetic world in a larger context, welding historical material, personal experience, and form into a unique whole. After Meyer's long years of groping experimentation, *Hutten* is indeed an amazing creative breakthrough.

The figure of Ulrich von Hutten (1488–1523) had been familiar to Meyer from his youth. Many writers of the 1840s praised Hutten as a model of fighting defiantly with both sword and pen for the cause of freedom. For the historical Hutten freedom primarily meant independence of German thought and politics from the supremacy of papal Rome. The religious and theological aspects of Luther's reformation mattered less to him. The politically oriented writers of the 1840s interpreted Hutten as a hero of individual freedom from the repressive state power of the Metternich restoration, and in the 1860s and 1870s he came to symbolize the will for German national unity and power. Meyer knew the Hutten poems by Georg Herwegh and Gottfried Keller as well as other contemporary works about Hutten.[1] The German knight was close to Meyer for another reason, too: the Zurich reformer Huldrych Zwingli had procured a peaceful exile for Hutten, then a sick and outlawed man, on the island of Ufenau in the lake of Zurich, where he died in the summer of 1523 after a short stay.

It is, however, characteristic for Meyer that this familiarity with

52

such timely material remained for a long time unproductive. As an historian by inclination Meyer always gathered and stored historical knowledge, but only considerably later did he recognize in it the poetic idea which would organize the material in such a way as to link it to his own experiences. In the case of Hutten it was the vision of the knight's lonely death on an island far removed from his former life of action. In the exiled Hutten Meyer could externalize his own feelings of being misunderstood and cut off from a full active life — feelings which were so painfully real that the poet recoiled from expressing them in his own name. At the same time, Hutten's past life embodied that other impetuously involved existence which was so far from Meyer's own experience but which, for this very reason, exerted an intriguing and troubling fascination on him. Most of the existential contrasts — so characteristic for his later works — are outlined here on a broader scale than that of the earlier ballads. In addition to the basic contrast between a life of almost unlimited action and one marked by confinement and death there are the conflicts wtihin the active life: epicurean enjoyment of life is confronted with problematical responsibility, the world of the Italian Renaissance is pitted against that of the German Reformation, preluding the later contrast between a world of aesthetic beauty and that of the pure word of ethics or religion.

But before all this could be integrated into a larger work Meyer labored for concept and form. At the beginning he only envisaged a poem describing Hutten's death. The first of these so-called "nucleus poems" (*Keimgedichte*) is entitled "Sterben im Frühlicht" ("Death at Sunrise") and was written as early as 1866 (*W*, VIII, 236–37). On his deathbed Hutten voices his deep desire not to die at night but at sunrise surrounded by the signs and symbols of new life; in changed metrical form this poem later became part of *Hutten* under the title "Scheiden im Licht" ("Departing in the Light"). Not until 1870 did the poet take up the motif again, writing five versions of a poem "Der sterbende Hutten" ("The dying Hutten,"(*W*, VIII, 239–53) which he describes in his essay "Mein Erstling Huttens letzte Tage" as follows: "Among my poetic plans there was a sketch in which the sick knight looks into the dying sunset while a Holbeinian death figure cuts a golden grape from the vine in the arched window. This sketch meant: 'Ripeness is all.' This is the nucleus from which my Hutten originated" (*W*, VIII, 193–94).[2] Here, the emphasis is shifted: Hutten's life symbolized by a ripe grape is harshly cut by death. Yet the last stanza expresses the hope that Hutten's example will continue to live as a spiritual stimulation for future generations.

In the nucleus poems Meyer experiments not only with ideas, individual words or lines, but also with metrical forms. The three-stress dactyls of 1866, which create a melody too soft for the stark contrast of death and rising sun, are exchanged for the heavier tro-chaic meter with four and then even five stresses; the rhymes of the four-line stanza vary between *a b a b* and *a b b a*. Such relatively small changes indicate the poet's dissatisfaction as well as his dogged groping for a really creative fusion of form and content. A decisive change occurs in the last nucleus poem when Meyer chooses a completely new stanza — a five-stress iambic couplet with a masculine rhyme. Although a Platen poem written in this form had been pointed out to Meyer as an example among others for a more concise style his choice of this rarely used stanza is a creative act in its own right, because he instinctively grasped the full potential of this form for the Hutten theme. By being concise, even abrupt, it fits Hutten's way of taking fast, uncompromising actions; by having a binary structure it lends itself well to express-ing the contrasts so essential for the theme; and the iambic meter — unlike the earlier and heavier trochaic one — provides just enough suppleness to convey a discreet lyricism in Hutten's feelings. This change in form is complemented by a shift in perspective and con-tent: as in the first poem Hutten speaks himself, thus the poem gains greater immediacy of expression. Sitting in a boat Hutten is now absorbed in contemplating the young face of his boatman and his own furrowed one — both reflected in the calm water of the lake. Reflection in the literal and figurative sense turns out to be a main element for the larger work.

With the new stanza Meyer acquires his own particular tone. Yet the effect of this "formal" discovery goes even further: after having found the form congenial to the content the Hutten poem suddenly expands into a verse cycle. Once the form was assured Meyer was able to exploit the rich possibilities of the material. In other words, the form assumes a creative energy by stimulating Meyer's imagination and, as is evident in the development of many poems, by providing him with a firm framework within which to express his deepest and often unsettling thoughts. Establishing the form is of special importance for Meyer's works in general; in the case of *Hutten,* it is one of the elements favoring the surprisingly fast creation of a larger work: within less than a year the cycle of fifty-four poems was completed.[3]

There were, of course, other favorable elements. In his essay on Hutten Meyer lists his own experience of inner exile, his love for the lake and its landscape, which he always felt to be congenial to him, and the "force of great historical events," that is, the Franco-Prussian War and the unification of Germany (*W,* VIII, 192). Yet as indicated earlier[4] his enthusiasm for a domineering Prussian Germany was not as wholehearted as he presented it. Meyer's feelings toward the newly emerging state were probably divided between a certain fascination with victorious power, a hope for an improved governmental form, and deep doubts about naked power and German depreciation of French culture. Yet if he wanted to avoid "being walled in" completely in Zurich — as he wrote to Mathilde Wesendonck in early 1871 (*W,* VIII, 157) — he had to profess more emotional partisanship for Germany than he really felt. Despite its immediacy of expression and its rapid completion *Hutten* is therefore much less the product of soaring emotions than of complicated feelings and circumstances. Before turning to the work itself a word must be said about its different editions. When almost ten years after the second edition of 1872 Haessel planned a third one in 1881, Meyer thoroughly revised and even enlarged the work from fifty-four to seventy-five poems. These were subsequently reduced to seventy-one in the fifth edition of 1884. More changes were made in the sixth to eighth editions (1887–1891) though decreasing in number and importance. For our discussion the edition of 1891 will serve as basis because it is now considered as the representative text.[5]

Two momentous events form the frame of the work: Hutten's landing on the island of Ufenau and his death, pictured as his departure in Charon's boat. Between these points, which are fairly close in time, the poet unfolds Hutten's past and present life as the exiled knight experiences it in daily impressions, dramatic memories, and lyric meditations. The series of loosely strung poems is held together by the unified viewpoint of Hutten speaking in the first person and by a prevailing elegiac mood of a man who loved the struggles and pleasures of life and who is now doomed to death. Despite dramatic elements the work lacks continuous, unifying action and is thus basically lyrical.

Huttens letzte Tage is divided into eight parts differing in length from four to seventeen poems. A closer look at these parts and their content, however, reveals a symmetrical arrangement in the sense that the first and the last part, the second and the seventh, etc., correspond to each other as reflecting images. The first part "Die Ufenau" ("The Ufenau") focuses on Hutten's arrival on this island which is unfamiliar to him, while the last part, "Das Sterben" ("Death"), focuses on his departure to the unknown land of death. But the corresponding features extend even further: when settling in on the Ufenau, Hutten surrounds himself with his pen and sword, his only possessions, and his host, a Catholic priest and doctor, furnishes him with the Dürer engraving "Ritter, Tod und Teufel" ("Knight, Death, and Devil"). These are the symbols of his life, and they recall his fight against what he conceived as wrong ideas. He still hopes to get better, to take at least an intellectual part in the great controversies of the time, although in "Consultation" his host advises him to abstain from all such excitement. Hutten then summarizes this advice in a poignant couplet: "Freund, was du mir verschreibst, ist wundervoll: / *Nicht* leben soll ich, wenn ich leben soll!" ("Friend, what you prescribe for me is wondrous: / I should *not* live if I am to live!"). In the last part, death has become a certainty for Hutten, and thus, he is concerned with his spiritual possessions. In contemplating the crucifix, his pains are alleviated ("Das Kreuz," "The Cross"), he finds comfort in words by Saint Paul and by Socrates ("Ein christliches Sprüchlein," "Ein heidnisches Sprüchlein"; "A Christian Proverb," "A Pagan Proverb"). His fight against death has been replaced by an acceptance of it which enables him to view his short life positively ("Die Traube," "The Grape"), and personal hope for recovery is superseded by hope for a better future which is symbolized by the rising sun ("Scheiden im Licht," "Departing in the Light").

The second part, "Das Buch der Vergangenheit" ("The Book of the Past"), recalls crucial episodes from Hutten's past presenting historical figures as well as his own actions. There are his scathing tirades against the Roman Church and her scorn of German culture ("Romfahrt," "Pilgrimage to Rome") and against the selling of indulgences ("Die Ablassbude," "Booth for Indulgences"); and there is the memory of his fiery pamphlets which led to his falling out with his parents and his final separation from the family ("Jacta est alea," "The Die is Cast"). The reminiscence of his and his friends' youthful mockery of debauched monks in "Epistolae obscurorum virorum" ("The Letters of the Dark Men") ends on a bitter note:

Als wir im losen Mummenschanz getobt,
Da hat man unsres Witzes Salz gelobt;

Doch als die Wahrheit wir im Ernst gesagt,
Da wurden wir, die Jäger, selbst gejagt.

When we ran wild in loose mummery,
The salt of our wit was praised;

But when we spoke the truth in earnest,
We, the hunters, became the hunted.

And while criticizing the old-fashioned Bayard, the "knight without fear and reproach," Hutten realizes that if Bayard lived in an already lost past he himself could look equally ridiculous for living in and for a future which is still far off: "Wir sind ein fahrend Ritterpaar, Bayard, / Und taugen beide nicht zur Gegenwart" ("We are a pair of knights errant, Bayard, / Both of us not fit for the present").

In this second part Meyer focuses on the problematic external situation of the reformer, and in the seventh "Dämonen" ("Demons"), he shows the internal side of this experience. Assailed by tormenting doubts, it is difficult for the sick man not to lose his belief in the justification of his cause, and in God's justice ("Herzog Ulrich," "Duke Ulrich"). In "Sturm und Schilf" ("Sedge in Storm"), he hears the devil mocking him as a fool fighting for clouds, and he sees his mother lamenting the fact that he not only destroyed the happiness of old times but also forfeited his salvation. Having withstood the attacks of these doubts he is gratified by a vision of mankind's rise into the light ("Die Menschheit," "Mankind"). Thus, in the inertia of his exile Hutten has to struggle with deep anxieties.

The third part "Einsamkeit" ("Solitude") unites a variety of poems mainly concerning Hutten's human nature and his favorite ideas. Here we find the forceful poem "Homo sum" ("I am Human") in which Hutten describes the many contradictions in his attitudes, concluding with the famous couplet which Meyer used as a motto for the work: "...ich bin kein ausgeklügelt Buch, / Ich bin ein Mensch mit seinem Widerspruch" ("I am no subtly contrived book, / I am a man with his contradictions"). Thinking about astrology prompts him to reaffirm his basic belief in individual freedom: "Du bist ein Feind von jeder Tyrannei / Und deine Sünden auch begingst du frei" ("You are a foe of every tyranny, /

And even your sins you committed freely''). When reading Ariost, Hutten reluctantly admits the value of elegant, ironic art and recognizes the limits of his own poetic endeavors. In ''Die Vorrede'' (''Preface'') he proudly confesses that his attack on the pope was just cause for his proscription while the following poem, ''Erasmus,'' shows his melancholy and bitterness about the humanist's refusal to take sides openly. Poems full of admiration for Luther and his Bible translation are followed by ''Deutsche Libertät'' (''German Liberty'') and ''Der Schmied'' (''The Blacksmith'') which formulate Hutten's hope for Germany's freedom. Here Meyer paid his — varying — tribute to the idea of a powerful German state: ''Der Schmied'' added to the third edition of *Hutten* is a toned-down version of an 1870 poem in which Meyer unambiguously declared his feelings for Germany and against France; by doing so he had — so to speak — set up his German mask.[6] Behind this mask he felt freer to express more balanced, democratic ideas: ''Deutsche Ritterschaft'' (''German Knighthood'') in the first and second editions, for instance, contains the vision that in a free Germany class distinctions would be abolished and the whole people would be knighted.[7] In 1881, this latter poem was given a more nationalistic ring while the former was depoliticized. This development shows how far Meyer was from committing himself to narrow, fixed ideas.

Limitations of Hutten's nature are exposed in the third part; the corresponding sixth part, ''Das Todesurteil'' (''Death Sentence''), is concerned with the ultimate limitation of death when the famous doctor Paracelsus crushes all hope for Hutten's recovery. Isolation from action now becomes isolation from life. Grieving over a future cruelly cut short Hutten regrets not having participated more decisively in past battles (''Die Beichte,'' ''Confession''):

> Mich reut mein allzu spät erkanntes Amt!
> Mich reut, dass mir zu schwach mein Herz geflammt!
>
> Mich reut, dass ich in meine Fehden trat —
> Mit schärfern Streichen nicht und kühnrer Tat!
>
> I regret having realized my duty all too late!
> I regret that my heart burned all too weakly!
>
> I regret that I did not engage in my feuds
> With sharper blows and more courageous deeds!

Yet nature, with her first autumnal tints, teaches him to accept this early end ("Das fallende Laub," "Falling Leaves") and to recognize the beauty of ripeness for which death is natural fulfillment. While Part 3 focuses on Hutten's position in life, Part 6 emphasizes his separation from life.

The fourth and fifth parts are the only ones that show the exiled knight in contact with the outside world. In Part 4, "Huttens Gast" ("Hutten's Guest") this world is represented by Loyola, the founder of the Jesuit order, who stops on the island on his pilgrimage to Jerusalem. Once again Hutten is confronted with the absolute power which Catholicism wants to exert on human souls. A glimpse at Loyola's nocturnal flagellation and his ardent prayer to the Virgin fills him with a horrible premonition of future religious battles. This encounter with a towering representative of an absolute power is followed, in the fifth part, "Menschen" ("People"), by encounters with simple people — peasants and soldiers. In small matters dogmatic attitudes appear as destructive ("Die Bilderstürmer," "The Iconoclasts"; "Schweizer und Landsknechte," "Swiss and Lansquenets"), and finally conversations with the island's priest about Copernicus outline a new view of the world which makes absolute religious pronouncements ever more questionable ("Nachtgespräch," "Nocturnal Converse"; "Der Pfarrer," "The Parish Priest").

In these middle sections of the work, Meyer describes Hutten's contacts with the world; but these contacts are mere shadows of the spontaneous involvement and forceful action which filled his earlier life. Position and content of the parts mirror his exile situation: what used to be his entire existence — active confrontation — has dwindled to incidental contacts whose consequences are of a purely contemplative nature. And this last remnant of his earlier life is surrounded by meditation. The importance of this symmetry is also borne out by the fact that Meyer strengthened it in the revision of 1881 by reducing the initial nine to eight parts despite an increase in the number of poems.

Such a strictly symmetrical form heightens the effect which the lack of any external action creates: Hutten's life is already at an end. On the island he is literally and figuratively isolated from the mainstream of events, isolated from the changing life traditionally symbolized by the running water of a brook or stream. He is surrounded by the calm, stagnant water of the lake in which his life is reflected. The visual image for such reflection in the fullest sense of the word is offered in the poem "Der kleine Ferge" ("The Young Boatman"), which is derived from the last nucleus poem:

Lass, Ruodi, deinen Nachen sachter gehn!
In klare Gründe lass mich niedersehn!

Hier im kristallnen Spiegel farbenmild
Erscheint ein Mann und eines Knaben Bild.

Du schaust empor in Ringellockenzier,
Vor zwanzig Sommern, Knabe, glich ich dir.

Und noch ein ander Bildnis schaut empor,
Das tief gefurchte kommt bekannt mir vor!

Nun, diese schwer beschriebne Stirn ist mein —
Fürwahr, ich möchte nicht ein andrer sein!

Ruodi, let the boat go more gently!
Let me look down into clear depths!

Here in the crystal mirror, in mild colors,
Appear the images of a man and a boy.

You look up in the beauty of your curls,
Twenty summers ago I resembled you.

And yet another image gazes upward,
The deeply wrinkled one seems familiar to me!

Well, this forehead, heavily inscribed, is mine —
Truly, I wouldn't want to be another man!

In the absence of any external action Hutten's situation undergoes only an internal change: his political exile intensifies to an exile from life, while meditation and the approaching death deepen the meaning of Hutten's past and present experiences. Instead of action in linear progression we witness a vertical deepening of images. For this reason, Meyer neglects temporal and causal connections between the individual poems so that they become almost separate entities, each one being concerned with only one event or motif. The poet presents Hutten's life — his active past and his contemplative last days — as a series of individual moments. Such a way of presentation is favored by Meyer's general inclination to view the past in fixed images or scenes. The result is a poetic practice which the poet himself outlines in the Hutten poem "Der Zecher" ("The Toper") of the first two editions (later shortened and entitled "Der letzte Humpen," "The Last Tankard"):

> Vor meinem fessellosen Geiste ziehn
> Des Rheines Wogen mit Gesang dahin.
>
> Ein werdend Lied taucht aus des Stromes Lauf
> Wie eine Fei mit hellen Augen auf.
>
> Doch eh' ich meinen Fang ans Land gerafft,
> Erhebt ein zweites schon sich nixenhaft,
>
> Winkt lachend mir mit beiden Armen zu:
> Ich bin das schönere, *mich* dichte du!
>
> Indes ich sinne, welches schöner sei,
> Entflieht die eine mit der andern Fei.

(*W,* VIII, 480)

> Before my unfettered spirit
> The waves of the Rhine pass a-singing.
>
> An emerging song rises from the stream
> Like a fairy with bright eyes.
>
> But before having hauled my catch to the shore,
> Another song appears like a mermaid,
>
> Laughingly beckons to me with both arms:
> I am the prettier one, compose *me!*
>
> While reflecting which one is the prettier
> The one fairy escapes with the other.

Meyer does what Hutten fails to do: in his writing he grasps at isolated motifs emerging from the vast material of history and life. Individual moments, key scenes, and symbols capture his imagination, not the continuous flow of time or the gradual development of events. The verse cycle about Hutten is a consistent application of this principle which accounts for the unusual flexibility of the work. Therefore, Meyer could insert new poems and remove old ones without basically altering the work as a whole. For this reason, it is also permissible to speak of *Hutten* without constantly referring to and differentiating between the various editions. This form of presenting a life or story in a series of insular moments becomes a characteristic feature of Meyer's novellas; and the discussion of his poetry will have to return to the above-mentioned method of separating one symbol from a larger context. Thus, the form is important not just for *Hutten* but for Meyer's subsequent prose and poetry.

From the very beginning, *Huttens letzte Tage* has been received positively, often enthusiastically, and it is to this day one of Meyer's most popular works. But its interpretation was often characterized by one-sided views which considered Hutten a simple advocate of German nationalism and as a representative of a deep Protestant belief. While some poems contain evidence for such an interpretation, others raise doubts about such absolute positions. For an appreciation of the whole work both sides must be taken into account; only in doing so can we assess Meyer's artistic achievement. He wanted to portray the historical Hutten, the rugged swordsman who was more interested in fighting than in theology; but, at the same time, he wanted to present this man at the close of his life as becoming aware of the intricacies of his former attitudes. By choosing Hutten's last days as a frame, Meyer created the possibility of showing Hutten in impetuous partisan action as well as in questioning reflection. In other words, the historical Hutten, the woodcut — so to speak — is combined with a more modern man, a more subtly shaded painting. Meyer lets the two coexist, leaving it up to the reader whether to be content with a one-sided, clear-cut view or to notice the significance of doubts. The loose sequence of poems and the symmetry support this double objective which allowed Meyer to capture his German public without having to subscribe fully to the narrow values of the day.

II   Engelberg

Hutten's immediate success at home and in Germany elated Meyer; the poem "Gloriola" ("A Little Laurel Wreath") added to *Hutten* in 1881 eloquently expresses this joy:

> Manch Kränzlein hab' ich später noch erjagt,
> Wie dieses erste hat mir keins behagt;
>
> Denn Süssres gibt es auf der Erde nicht
> Als ersten Ruhmes zartes Morgenlicht.
>
> Many a laurel wreath did I later win;
> But none pleased me better than this first one,
>
> For there is no sweeter thing on earth
> Than the delicate morning light of first fame.

It is no wonder that he was eager to write another work. A summer stay in the mountains of Davos revived old poetic ideas evoked long years ago by the beauty of the Alpine landscape in the Engelberg valley. In the fall of 1871 he set out to write *Engelberg* which would poetically embody "the soul of this Alpine valley," as the motto says. During its composition, another, quite different impulse affected Meyer's imagination: his encounter with the paintings of Titian — especially the Assunta — and of Giovanni Bellini in Venice where he spent the winter months of 1871-1872. Charm of Alpine scenery, the poetic name of Engelberg — Angel's Mountain — and Italian art thus contributed to the shaping of the verse narrative *Engelberg.*

Unlike Meyer's other works, this one contains only a few historical touches referring to Rudolf of Habsburg and his election to Emperor in 1291. Though the tale is set in a historically defined period, it is of a legendary quality and was freely invented by Meyer. In a letter to Haessel of February 27, 1872 he describes it: "...in accordance with the name Engelberg [the legend] treats, in transparent symbolism, a typical fate of a woman, a kind of medieval Psyche.... It shows the formation of a beautiful female character through earthly life" (*W,* IX, 100). This idea is couched in the following story. A little angel lost from the heavenly host of St. Cecilia is found in the mountains and brought up under the name of Engel or Angela in the nunnery of the village Engelberg. Her quiet life as the nunnery's doorkeeper is shattered by the suicide of her mistress Jutta, a young noblewoman who had been betrayed by her lover and forced to become a nun. Burdened with the guilt of having left Jutta unguarded for some moments, Engel escapes into the mountains where she meets a hunter who leads a solitary life, because he was exiled from his home country for his involvement in a bloody feud between two families. Engel and Kurd share their guilt feelings; they get married and live far from the village in the mountains. In an attempt to protect the flock of sheep Kurd is killed by a vulture, and Engel returns to the village with her four sons, who bring her both gratification and sorrow: one becomes a priest, another a rich merchant; the youngest one is an accomplished wood-carver but dies very young, and the oldest, a soldier as daring and impetuous as his father, drowns when trying to save his beloved and her smaller sisters from a flash flood. Having experienced life's fullest joys and deepest sorrows, Engel has become a mature woman respected by all. When asked to go and comfort a widow in the mountains, she ascends higher and

higher, finally rejoining the angels she had left so long ago. She is
greeted with the words:

> Dein Erdentag ist Dir zerronnen
> Doch hast Du durch die Glut der Schmerzen
> Auf ewig jetzt Gestalt gewonnen:
> Du kommst zurück mit einem Herzen.

(W, IX, 408)

> Your earthly day has vanished,
> But in the violence of your pains
> You have won human form for eternity: .
> You come back with a heart.

After having completed this truly legendary version in Venice,
Meyer felt compelled to make significant changes in the direction
of a more realistic plot. The story of Engel's descent from heaven is
shown as a pious lie used by the monk who wants to provide an
orphan girl with a home in the nunnery. But he knows — and later
tells Engel — that she is the illegitimate child of a proud woman
who had murdered her husband and made a servant her lover and
master of her estate. The servant, a hard and unjust man, was
killed, and the woman had to escape into the mountains, where she
died in childbirth, expressing her will that the child be reared in a
nunnery far from the world and its dangers. Engel's ascension to
heaven at the end is now seen as a symbolic return to her spiritual
home.

Despite extensive revisions the work was speedily completed and
appeared in August, 1872: Meyer seems to have followed up the
élan of the *Hutten* production. Yet the reactions to *Engelberg* were
mixed, and in Meyer's lifetime the work went through only five editions between 1872 and 1898. Meyer's own insecurity with regard to
it is expressed in several ways. On August 3, 1872 he wrote to
Vulliemin: "Honestly, I don't know whether I have written a pro-
found or a childish [*albern*] work" (*W,* IX, 104), and in the 1880s
he used to refer to the work in the diminutive as "Engelbergchen."
Scholars, in their turn, have characterized it as conventional, lacking an individual style and a clear concept. In Meyer scholarship
the work has been largely ignored, with the exception of Alfred
Zäch who, in connection with his editing the *Engelberg*-volume for
the historical-critical edition, carefully analyzed it in the context
both of the contemporary genre of the verse narrative and of

Meyer's other writings.[8] While he does not reach a different conclusion with regard to the work's aesthetic value, he focuses on those of its features which are of interest in connection with Meyer's style in general.

The change in plot outlined above indicates one of the main problems which faced the author. The pure simplicity of the Alpine landscape, the pious ardor of Titian's Assunta, and the graceful charm of the Bellini angels all drew Meyer to a world of elevated ideas and simple beauty. The legend, with its emphasis on spiritual significance over realistic portrayal, seemed best suited for embodying the idea of an angel's earthly life and her return to heaven as a soul both human and angelic. But even in this first legendary version Meyer added such troubling shadows as Jutta's suicide and Kurd's murderous hate. When replacing Engel's direct descent from heaven by her birth from proud and sinful parents, Meyer not only created greater realism but also drew on motifs which are dominant in his own thinking and which, in connection with the Jutta episode, he called his "original sources (*Urwasser*): love, hate, conscience" (*W,* IX, 98–99). However, against this dark and more realistic background the monk's tale about the lost angel assumes a questionable quality, and Engel's ascension to heaven at the end seems artificial.

Meyer's realism and the motifs of sinful love, hate, conscience, and death run counter to the simple spirituality of the legendary concept; but these elements prompted most of those passages which still impress readers of *Engelberg* with their poetic vigor and originality. Based on precise observation, the landscape descriptions attest to Meyer's striking ability to infuse an often unpretentious image with a natural yet exquisite beauty and significance. This is the case when, in Part 6, Engel and Kurd watch on a brilliant spring day the thawing of a mountain pond. Rigid old forms melt with the ice, making room for the flowing water, for new forms of life, and the first butterfly of the season seems to embody the young people's delicate, newborn love:

> Rings schwebt die stille Mittagshitze,
> Durch frischen Bergeshauch gekühlt.
> Sie kosen auf dem Felsensitze,
> Von neugeborner Flut umspült.
> Ein lichter Falter kommt geflogen,
> Vom Duft des Kranzes angezogen.

Und auf den jungen Nacken setzt
Er sich mit bebenden Schwingen jetzt.

The quiet noonday heat hovers round about,
Cooled by the fresh mountain air,
They caress on the rocky seat,
Laved round by the newborn surge.
A bright butterfly comes winging,
Attracted by the fragrance of the wreath,
And on the young neck he now alights
With trembling wings.

With only a few exceptions — Jutta's arrival in the monastery (Part 3) and young Kurd's death (Part 11) — the landscape is shown in radiant sunlight. But Meyer contrasts this external luminosity with deep shadows darkening the protagonists' internal existence. Jutta's life is so engulfed by darkness, hate, and even despair that only death can free her for another world. Meyer's crucial motif of the renegade monk[9] is here given a dramatic, desperate form. Even Engel, who had felt secure and content in the regulated monastic life, recognizes with horror that its calm order may bring death instead of spiritual life.

Death is prevalent throughout the work. Engel's husband and her oldest son meet an untimely death when engaged in fighting powers of nature in order to ensure protection for domestic life. Such occurrences also emphasize the threatening side of nature. The short life of Engel's youngest son, the gentle and sensitive artist, is marked by death not only in Werner's weak physical condition but — more importantly — in his early, indelible memory of his mother lost in grief over his dead father. In contrast to this art for which death is the deepest source, Meyer introduces an Italian artist who tries — in vain — to lure Werner to Italy. The description of the South in Part 10 is a jewel: in melodious verses Meyer combines his own symbols — ripe fruit, sail — with a Goethean radiance of light and colors.

Dort rauscht es in den Lorbeerhainen,
Dort lispelt des Ölbaums Silberblatt,
Dort ragt, aus ruhmberedten Steinen
Gefügt, manch marmorhelle Stadt.
Dort wogt der Markt von lautem Volke,
Dort wird der Himmel ohne Wolke,

Wo Zinne schwebt und Kuppel thront,
Von Götterbildern still bewohnt.
Dort spielt das Licht durch alle Räume,
Reift Frucht an Frucht der Sonne Glut
Und Segel ziehn wie helle Träume
Durch purpurdunkle Meeresflut.

There, there is a rustling in the laurel grove,
There, there is a whispering of the olive tree's silver leaf,
There, joined together out of panegyric stones,
Many a city, bright in marble, looms.
There the market place surges with noisy people,
There, where the cornice hovers and the dome is enthroned,
The cloudless sky is quietly inhabited by images of gods.
There the light pervades all spaces,
Fruit upon fruit is ripened in the glowing sun
And sails float on like bright dreams
Through the wine-dark surging sea.

Although Meyer intended *Engelberg* to be free from reflection, he could not check his innate tendency to probe life's dark depths. This resulted in a basically realistic approach to life, which was, however, not attuned to the genre Meyer chose here. In his analysis of nineteenth century verse narrative Zäch points out the following characteristic features: its topics lie in a historical or legendary world remote from reality and realistic description; its outlook on life, rooted in a yet untroubled confidence in civilization, is unflinchingly optimistic; and its graceful form is of prime importance. Clearly, the verse narrative was the preferred genre of a reading public for whom literature constituted a realm of serene beauty and of a cheerful view of life.

This educated bourgeoisie was actually the public which Meyer as a *Bildungsdichter* mainly addressed. And his story of the angel lost in an earthly life corresponds basically to the legendary quality of the verse narrative. But Meyer's realism in rendering the dark sides of life belong to a more complicated world. These typically Meyerian features could not be integrated into the traditional form of the verse narrative which Meyer kept both in meter — the four-stress rhymed iambics — and in basic concept; and thus, the work remains heterogenous and, despite beautiful passages, unsatisfying as a whole.

In a negative way, *Engelberg* demonstrates the importance of form for Meyer's writings. Since he was an outsider who was not really in tun. with the main trends of his time, the choice of such a traditional and rather simple form was problematic in itself. In addition, Meyer did not develop or vary the form as he changed both concept and content. Because this unchanged form was little suited for Meyer's more complex views it could not support, much less stimulate, his imagination to create a more differentiated content. Yet it seems as if the failure of *Engelberg* emphasized the accomplishment of *Hutten* — the development of a form which fully corresponds to his particular style. And when he set out to write prose works he had learned his lesson: not only did he choose a genre more suitable for his problematic themes but he adapted and varied the novella in such ways as to transform it into a perfect mirror of his ambiguous position.

CHAPTER 4

The Ambiguous Hero

A look at Meyer's larger works planned and written between 1866 and 1877 shows that the Reformation and the ensuing religious wars figured foremost in his mind. Starting in 1866 he devoted much time and effort to a work on the *Graubünden* political figure Jürg Jenatsch and his role in the Thirty Years War. But before completing this work in 1874 he finished two other Reformation works — *Huttens letzte Tage* and a novella *Das Amulett (The Amulet)* which focuses on the massacre of Saint Bartholomew in Paris in 1572. And after having revised *Jürg Jenatsch* for the book edition in 1876 he wrote another short novella set against the background of the Thirty Years War entitled *Der Schuss von der Kanzel (The Shot from the Pulpit).*

Meyer's preference for themes from these times was especially strong in this early period of his productive writing, but it never completely abated, as is evidenced by the novella *Gustav Adolfs Page (Gustav Adolf's Page)* and the never completed plans for two other prose works *Der Komtur (The Commander),* conceived in the later 1870s and dealing with Zwingli's reformation, and *Die sanfte Klosteraufhebung (The Gentle Secularization),* conceived in the 1880s. The psychologist A. Kielholz links Meyer's emphasis on the Reformation to a desire to surpass his father's historical studies about this period.[1] Since Meyer admired his father and, after his death, was continually exhorted to follow his example, it is certainly plausible that he would want to equal — if not to surpass — him at least in this one area. But an explanation of the phenomenon must also consider the attractions inherent in the material itself.

The sixteenth and seventeenth centuries were a period of transition, and it is this transitional character that most interested Meyer.

As early as September 5, 1866, he described to Haessel his fascination with the Jenatsch material in the following words: "The development — so extremely favorable to poetic effects — of a grand brutal period into a more civilized and shallower one, the change of the religious movement of the sixteenth century into a political one in the seventeenth, in short, the beginning of *modern* man would be interesting to treat" (*B*, II, 10). Inherent in this material are the possibilities for both dramatic effects involving power and convictions as well as for skeptical views questioning established concepts. The entangled conflicts of religious-political wars in a distant past allowed Meyer to describe extreme positions while enabling him to avoid taking sides openly. Unwilling to expose his skepticism directly, he had to find formal devices which would permit him to convey it in a covert way and without having to resort to direct authorial comments. *Hutten* offers a first solution: the hero's sickness and solitude warrant doubts, and by choosing the form of a fragmented monologue Meyer is able to hide his own views behind those of the protagonist. In the prose works, which had to be more dramatic and more panoramic, he solves the problem by using irony and framework stories.

I   Das Amulett

In 1873 Meyer published his first novella, *Das Amulett (The Amulet)*. Plans and historical studies for this work reach back to the years 1867–1869, but only after *Engelberg* were they taken up again and molded into a whole which already shows the basic complexity of form and content characteristic for Meyer's major novellas. While focusing mainly on middle-class people he shows them caught up in events of historical significance. By outlining the political situation in France and by introducing a row of historical figures — King Charles IX, his mother Catherine de Medici, the Protestant admiral and advisor to the King, Coligny, the writer Montaigne — Meyer demonstrates his ability to portray situations and characters with a few effective strokes. He has already found his style: for a complex material he chooses a concise yet ambiguous narration which heightens the dramatic effects of the story and deepens its irony.

On the surface, Meyer portrays strong beliefs. The Calvinist doctrine of predestination and Catholic Mariolatry rest on absolute faith in a divine power directly and meaningfully ruling the individual's life. Yet the inconclusive way of presenting such religious beliefs implicitly questions them and gives rise to a deep skepticism which despairs of any sense in either individual life or history. Most critics have given the work negative marks, calling it immature, equivocal, contrived, or blatantly fatalistic. Recent studies, however, convincingly show that ambiguity is an intentional device, and that the story as well as its form — a framework story with the principal character as the sole first-person narrator — are fitting expressions of Meyer's ironic intentions.[2] As David A. Jackson points out, this also calls for a change in assessing the significance of Prosper Mérimée's novel *Chronique du règne de Charles IX* (1829) for *Das Amulett*. Since Mérimée's depiction of events surrounding the St. Bartholomew Massacre is basically ironic, his influence must have transcended the realm of obvious and extensive plot similarities to which traditional criticism has restricted it.[3]

The Virgin Mary medallion mentioned in the title plays a pivotal role in exposing the story's basic question concerning the nature of fate. Boccard constantly wears this medallion in gratitude for his having been miraculously cured from a childhood paralysis by Our Lady of Einsiedeln. For him, the medallion is an amulet, the magic symbol of divine power to intervene directly in behalf of a faithful individual in distress. But in the course of events the medallion acquires an equivocal symbolism. When Schadau, in Chapter 6, duels Count Guiche, a high-born Catholic courtier and superior fencer, the medallion, which Boccard had secretly slipped into Schadau's jerkin, staves off Guiche's deadly thrust, thus saving the Protestant who violently rejects Boccard's belief in Mary as "reprehensible superstition" (*W*, XI, 48). But during the massacre, when Boccard helps to rescue Schadau's young wife Gasparde, the medallion fails to protect its faithful wearer, who had embarked on the dangerous venture with a prayer to Mary. Thus, the amulet turns into an inconclusive symbol that stands for such different meanings as the merciful power of Mary, Schadau's concept of predestination and, on a more encompassing level, an incomprehensible, capricious fate.

While the events obviously question Boccard's faith in Mary, they seem to give proof of the Calvinist doctrine of predestination. Schadau does not hesitate to regard his repeated salvation as predetermined by God. Meyer, however, far from sharing this view, criticizes it in an intrinsically ironic way without openly intruding into Schadau's role as narrator. It is, therefore, Schadau's narration itself which reveals questionable points — discrepancies between his thinking and acting, his conceived role and his actual performance, between reality and its interpretation. Thus, for all his straightforward simplicity Schadau turns out to be an ambiguous hero, and, in David Jackson's phrase, "a satirized narrator." As shown in Chapter 2, Schadau is not only a confirmed Calvinist by family tradition and education, he also boasts of his special liking of "the austere consistency of the Calvinist doctrine" (*W*, XI, 10). Yet when his own desires are at stake his principles fade: he easily discards his moral scruples with regard to Gasparde's illegitimate birth because he is dazzled by the possibility of wooing, perhaps proposing, to the daughter of his hero Dandelot (*W*, XI, 32–33); he excuses the heretic views of his uncle while rigorously condemning Servetus; and to enlist Boccard's help for Gasparde's rescue he uses what he abhors most in Catholicism — an invocation of Mary (*W*, XI, 64). At the same time, Meyer contrasts his dogmatic rigor with the human concern which tempers Chatillon's faith and which even transcends Boccard's Catholic prejudices.

The doubtful nature of Schadau's belief is reflected in other ways as well. The often criticized second chapter serves an essential function by demonstrating how the concept of predestination induces the young man to confound wishful thinking with presentiments of a heroic destiny. He sees himself not only as being involved in the "great destiny of the Protestant world" (*W*, XI, 14) but also as finding a bride in the environment of the admired Coligny, perhaps winning her in some daring way, as did his particular hero Dandelot (*W*, XI 15). While the Parisian events seem to fulfill these dreams of heroic action, Schadau is actually reduced to a rather passive role: he owes his position as Coligny's clerk to Chatillon's recommendation, his victory over Guiche to Boccard's medallion, and the rescue of his wife to Boccard's altruistic action. Moreover, the duel, his main combatant action, contributes to precipitating the massacre and thus is harmful to the cause that, sword in hand, he so fervently wanted to further. To Schadau, however, even incidental details — such as the thunderstorm in Chapter 3 — appear as necessary links in his preordained fate. One the basis of his belief that "the deity is omniscient and omnipotent, whatever it foresees and does not prevent is its will" (*W*, XI, 21), the mere sequence of events implies a judgment:Schadau's protection points to his being one of God's elect, Boccard's death to his inferiority as a Catholic.

In this context, the massacre scenes contain a scathingly ironic comment, since Schadau actually would have to accept the slaughter of his own people as God's will. But when, in Chapter 8, he catches a glimpse of the king and the queen mother, a very different view is presented. In describing the king's face as "[distorted] by fear, rage, madness to a hellish expression" and by calling Catherine de Medici "pale and motionless ... with an almost indifferent mien" (*W,* XI, 61), Meyer creates a powerful image of the real "gods" of history — human beings seized by wild emotions and wielding dreadful, impersonal power. Schadau's ensuing dream emphasizes the absurdity of a fight which only has to do with "the right way to heaven" (*W,* XI, 63), and not with problems of this life. Thought-provoking as the story's events are, they fail to effect a change in Schadau's attitude. While he has flashes of deeper insight — recognizing the human value of Boccard's friendship after the duel, and seeing, in reality and in his dream, the ungodly powers of history — he lacks any real development: David Jackson has rightly termed the work an "Antibildungsroman."[4] It is thus fitting that the story describes a geographical circle ending in the place where Schadau's concepts were formed and where he will spend the rest of his life. Moving in closed circles is characteristic of Schadau; and in order to show this Meyer provides his novella, in its first chapter, with a framework story which takes place in 1611, almost forty years after the St. Bartholomew Massacre. In a meeting with Boccard's old, lonely father, Schadau is, once again, confronted with his potentially disturbing memories; but despite being "tormented" by them he exonerates himself: "I dragged [Boccard] into death. And yet, as heavily as this weighs upon me, I cannot regret it, and today, in the same situation, I would have to act in the same way as I did at twenty" (*W,* XI, 8).

With this circular presentation Meyer gives his framework story a closed form which reflects Schadau's closed mind. This tight structure, however, produces an ambiguous effect: by setting up, on the surface, a definite view of life it actually gives ironic relief to a view of basic skepticism and uncertainty. The latter traits are, of course, the marks of the nineteenth century to which Meyer relates his sixteenth-century story by means of a fictional editorial comment that precedes the first chapter: "Old yellowed pages are lying before me covered with notes from the early seventeenth century. I am translating them into the language of our time." Translating here is to be understood in a wider sense as presenting history in such a way as to make it relevant to Meyer's modern readers. As Schimmelpfennig points out,[5] the early 1870s show many similarities with the sixteenth century: the movement to strengthen the pope's authority culminated in 1870 in the dogma of papal infallibility, and this, in turn, led to the anti-Catholic measures of the so-called *Kulturkampf* in Germany. Deeply concerned about religious — and national — prejudices, Meyer wanted to call attention to their inhuman consequences. In *Das Amulett* his sole purpose consists in exposing the devastating effects that absolute positions have had on minds, individuals and entire groups at all times.

II   Jürg Jenatsch

Once *Das Amulett* was finished, Meyer turned all his attention to the Jenatsch material again, and within about a year he completed a work which had occupied his mind for more than a decade.[6] But despite extensive historical studies and dedicated work — especially during 1866 and 1867 and in the winters of 1871–1872 and 1872–1873 — only little had been written down on paper. The speedy completion of this arduous project, therefore, seems to suggest that the shorter novella constituted necessary practice for dealing with historical themes. And a comparison of the two works leaves no doubt that with *Jürg Jenatsch* Meyer reached an indisputable mastery in effectively condensing vast historical materials into a work of dramatic intensity and complex meaning.

Among the preserved Jenatsch manuscripts there is a chronological list of the historical events concerning Georg — or Jürg — Jenatsch and the history of Graubünden or Bünden, a small independent mountain republic situated in the southeastern corner of present-day Switzerland. This list, reprinted in the Jenatsch volume of the historical-critical edition (*W,* X, 293–97),[7] provides an insight into the maze of political and religious struggles, large and small battles and treaties marking Graubünden's history between 1620 and 1639 when the country was not only racked by internal strife but had also become a pawn in the war calculations of France and the Hapsburg Empire. With regard to the main facts of Jenatsch's life, Meyer closely follows history, but he only selects a few key events for description. In the first part, he concentrates on the Valtelline massacre of 1620 which prompts Jenatsch to abandon the ministry and take up arms, and he summarizes Jürg's murder of the Catholic Pompejus Planta and his heroic fighting against the invading Spanish–Austrian troops in 1621. In the second part, Meyer focuses on the winter of 1634–1635 when Jenatsch in Venice joins the French army which, under the command of the Protestant duke of Rohan, is to free Graubünden from Spanish oppression; and in the third part he relates Jenatsch's betrayal of Rohan and the forced withdrawal of the French troops in 1637, his negotiations with Austria-Spain, his conversion to Catholicism, and his assassination in early 1639. Meyer combines these events with smaller incidents which are historical, but which are often shifted back or forth in time so as to heighten the suspense and to broaden the protagonist's image. For example, two separate incidents — Jenatsch's duel with his superior Ruinelli in 1627 and his imprisonment in Venice in 1630 — are made a part of what happens in the winter of 1634–1635. Rohan's death of 1638 is postponed and the ratification of Graubünden's treaty with Spain is antedated, so that both events coincide with the assassination of Jenatsch at a banquet in 1639 which, in Meyer's account, is the official celebration of his success.

The main deviation from history consists in the fact that, between Jenatsch and Planta's daughter Lucretia, Meyer creates a childhood bond which develops into a lifelong love. Lucretia, however, is torn between her love and her duty — considered sacred — to avenge her father; thus, she adamantly refuses Jenatsch while also deferring revenge on him. Yet when other people set out to kill him she steps in and slays him herself. The historical Catherine Planta was married and was merely present at the assassination. Meyer also adds a fictitious friendship between Jenatsch and Zurich's mayor Heinrich Waser, who historically played a role in Graubünden politics, but had no contact with Jenatsch. Even in his deviations Meyer lets his imagination be guided by details found in historical sources. As much as possible he remains within the realm of actual happenings in order to create a relatively firm ground for his personal view of Jürg Jenatsch as an intriguing hero and an exponent of the ambivalence of political action. It is reminiscent of Schiller's creation of Wallenstein when Meyer describes his Jenatsch with the words: "I am sure that Jenatsch was nothing but a scoundrel and I have made him a personality" (*B*, I, 128). Feeling still rather unsure of himself as an author, Meyer apparently needed a firm historical ground and thus also devoted much time — more than for any of the later works — to source readings. And in order to cover himself against possible criticism from historians he called the work "unhistorical."

Yet such excuses proved unnecessary. The work, first published serially in 1874 in the periodical *Die Literatur,* was a success. In Meyer's lifetime alone Haessel issued thirty editions, and to this day it is one of Meyer's most popular works. With vigorous strokes he created a hero of forceful vitality fascinating in his mixture of spontaneity and cold calculation. Dramatic suspense is carefully built up and maintained throughout the book, and the action takes place against a background that is diverse and colorful, but never distracting. There are precise yet evocative descriptions of locales — for instance, that of the summer day on the Julierpass at the opening of the book — and vivid sketches of a wide variety of minor characters — the jovial confectioner and former minister Lorenz Fausch, Planta's gruff and vengeful servant Lucas, the affable, clever Pater Pankraz, the pedantic historian Fortunatus Sprecher. All this attests to Meyer's increasing ability to create with economical means a rich world within a limited space.

The work is divided into three books entitled "The Trip of Mr. Waser," "Lucretia," and "The Good Duke." Since Jürg Jenatsch holds the reader's attention from beginning to end, the choice of these titles is at first surprising. A closer look at the structure of the entire work shows, however, that besides being major characters in the story, the three figures also function as contrasts to and partial illuminations of Jenatsch. Meyer uses the three parts to build up the complexity of Jenatsch's figure in a way reminiscent of the classical sonata form: in the first part a slow opening is followed by an explosion of events; the second part has little action, but provides multiple reflections of Jenatsch; and the third one is filled to overflowing with fast-moving events.

Taking place in 1620–1621, the first book centers on the beginning of Jürg's military and political career and on his fast rise, described in Chapter 7, to being a champion of independence of heroic stature, a "Graubünden Tell" who slew, in one instance, "hundreds of Austrians . . . in open battle, he alone with three companions" (*W,* 74). If this book stresses the heroic aspects of Jenatsch's actions, his heroism is nevertheless not without its dubious elements. Imperious and temerarious by nature he treats the problems of European politics so impetuously that, in Chapter 5, Waser is "frightened and upset by the brazenness with which Jürg recklessly cut the hard knots..." (*W,* 47). This impetuousity later characterizes his brutal murder of Pompejus Planta. The emotional depth of his nature is revealed when his young, beautiful wife Lucia is killed in the massacre: his adoration for her turns "into speechless wrath and implacable grief" (*W,* 63), and he turns "into stone" (*W,* 71). Spontaneous and forceful as he is, he easily falls prey to fanaticism, exceeds normal limits, and seems to defy every form. Heinrich Waser, the city person and future diplomat, sets a stark contrast. He is a man of form, cautiously curious and warily neutral, at every moment conscious of limits not to be overstepped. At once fascinated and frightened by Jürg's uncompromising vehemence, he is the observer, and as such Meyer repeatedly introduces him at crucial points throughout the story. Yet he is a negative character. As Karl Schmid convincingly shows, he is cunning, but weak, and his neutrality is rooted in fear and calculation.[8] In Waser, Meyer criticizes his native Zurich for her philistine morality and her petty caution, which he himself experienced time and again. Another native of Zurich, Rohan's adjutant Rudolf Wertmüller, corroborates this interpretation from the other side. Despite his whimsical behavior and his skepticism, he is a positive figure with a keen sense of justice and ethical values; thus, he feels nothing but contempt for Zurich's bourgeois pettiness.

In the second book, historical action is at a standstill, and the action on the personal level — Jenatsch's imprisonment and release, his meeting with Lucretia in Venice in the winter of 1634–1635 — is mainly designed to present the reader with various interpretations of the protagonist. In contrast to his earlier impetuous spontaneity Jürg now exhibits the confidence and smooth manners of a gentleman of the world. In a few instances, however, his vehemence of feeling comes to light again, most notably in Chapter 4: hearing Wertmüller's rather ironic account of how Lucretia warded off a crudely intruding suitor, his face freezes to "metallic hardness" and appears "strangely distorted and threatening in its torpor" (*W,* 110). Reminiscent of his reaction at the death of Lucia, this silent response signals the persistence of his attachment to Lucretia as well as of his emotional impetuosity. While Wertmüller wonders about Jenatsch "are you a hero or a buffoon?" (*W,* 103–4), the Venetian *provveditore* Grimani takes a devastating stance in Chapters 6 and 7. He sees Jürg as cultivating a "malicious art of presenting even the most intentional act as an inspiration of the moment or as an innocuous coincidence" (*W,* 127). Behind such calculation he detects an infinite ambition that would let him "recklessly tear down every barrier restraining this ambition. Ever·

barrier! Military obedience, a given word, the most sacred duty of gratitude!'' (*W,* 131). Waser and Rohan reject this view; the latter believes Jenatsch to be ''as wild and as honest as an element of nature'' (*W,* 131). Grimani's opinion also seems somewhat questionable because of his obvious dislike for Jenatsch whose vigorous nature sharply contrasts with the Venetian's cold, refined intellect. Nevertheless, Meyer induces the reader more and more to doubt Jürg's motivations by skillfully underpinning the negative opinions with subtler hints. There is, in Chapter 3, the remark that Waser had heard rumors about Jenatsch's ''frequent camp duels unexpectedly fatal for the often higher placed opponent'' (*W,* 98), a rumor corroborating Grimani's view. Or there is the ambiguous impression that Jürg first makes on Rohan, who is ''more pleased with the captivating warmth of the speaker than with his heavy flattery'' (*W,* 96).

This part, entitled ''Lucretia,'' also provides insight into the relation between her and Jenatsch when, in Chapter 5, they unexpectedly meet in Rohan's palace. Here Meyer brings them together for the first time as adults after having related only their childhood encounter in Zurich in Chapter 2 of the first book. Despite a lapse of about fifteen years, and despite all the religious, political, and personal barriers between them, they are still emotionally tied to each other. But because of Jürg's wild politics, climaxing in his murdering her father, this tie has become desperately double-edged for Lucretia. By refusing to make peace with him she insolubly ties the present to the past, and Jenatsch is faced with the fact that his future is burdened with a past which he now cursed ''as an unnecessary sullying of his hands'' (*W,* 150). Jenatsch submits his life to Lucretia: ''The decision rests with you, who ... has the greater claim on me, Graubünden or you?'' (*W,* 116–17). This sharpens their old dilemma, the incompatibility of personal desires and higher duties for both of them, thus dramatizing the personal background for the impending political development. This tightening of the link between the individual and the general, between internal and external history, is one reason for the second book's being entitled ''Lucretia.'' Another one is Lucretia herself. Although her part is quite limited, Meyer establishes her immediately as an unconventional figure of undaunted spirit, deep emotions, and singular strength of purpose. She is Jenatsch's equal in strength, but where his theatrical behavior stirs suspicions, hers is direct and unpretending.

In the third book the emphasis is on action, on historical events spanning the years 1635 to 1639. As the title "The Good Duke" indicates, it is Rohan who is Jürg's main counterpart here. In many ways he resembles Jenatsch: he is a Protestant, a soldier, and ingenious general, and he deeply loves Graubünden. Yet his actions are always kept in check by an absolute commitment to ethical values. By yielding to Jenatsch and keeping his terms for withdrawal, by refusing to resort to armed resistance he spares Graubünden — exhausted as she is — another bloodbath. As shown in Chapter 9, he preserves his honor, but has to stand the humiliating loss of his military and political reputation as well as of his fatherland: "If it is impossible for me to remain, at the same time, a Frenchman and a man of honor, ... I choose the latter even if I should become homeless" (*W,* 217). His death as a simple soldier on a German battlefield points to the ultimate basis for his values — a firm religious belief. In Rohan, Meyer creates a spiritual hero whose portrait is all the more moving and authentic, since he is equipped with a good sense for the realities of this imperfect world. He is clearly aware of the possibility that the ruthless Cardinal Richelieu might take advantage of his very loyalty to ethical principles. His foible — characteristic also of the historical Rohan — is a human one, namely, his unshakeable trust in Jenatsch. Yet combined with failure — even failure to defend his principles actively — Rohan's attitude is not beyond any doubt, and his epithet "the good duke" assumes a slightly ironic ring.

Although successful in his undertakings, Jenatsch now becomes an increasingly negative figure: the suspicions voiced earlier are shown to be justified. At the same time, Meyer takes care not to degrade him too much in order to keep the reader's judgment in suspense. During Rohan's campaign, described in the second chapter, he appears as a shining hero. Even the skeptical Wertmüller comes to admire his "daring [which] appeared boundless and yet [was] circumspect" (*W,* 154), and Rohan is pleased by his acceptance of rigorous discipline. But this submission to limits set by principles is swept away when Jenatsch realizes that Richelieu indeed misuses Rohan's integrity in order to deceive Graubünden, which he intends to keep as a pawn for France's future power calculations. In the pivotal fifth chapter, Rohan appears as a gullible, duped "Christian knight" (*W,* 176), a doomed man, and Graubünden's freedom seems to vanish forever. All this results for Jenatsch in a sudden inversion of values: "Down with the past!

Away with its shackles of treasured convictions and prejudices! Severed be every bond of gratefulness and loyalty!" (*W,* 177). In this new order, the concern for freedom assumes absolute priority, ruse justifies ruse, and Jürg's entire ambition is set loose, roused by the prospect of his duping Richelieu with the cardinal's own means. Therefore, it is not surprising that Jenatsch starts to transgress any limit in his way. Openly coveting Lucretia, he reveals in Chapter 11 his hubris: "I swear to you, Lucretia, if I succeed in this [his negotiations with Spain] nothing shall be impossible for me any more! ... even if I had to wade through the blood of your father!" (*W,* 227). Lulled into security by success and seeming impunity he fails to realize that his further transgressions — his conversion to Catholicism as well as his disregard for the rules of the political power play vis-à-vis Spain's Serbelloni — become destructive: Lucretia decides to take the veil, Serbelloni resolves to have him assassinated, and Jenatsch falls prey to self-destructive hubris: "I have reached my goal and would like to say, 'I am tired,' had not a demon laid hold of me, lashing me to go forward into the unknown, into the void!" (*W,* 256).

Jenatsch's death has become inevitable, and the complexities of his life climax in the scene of his assassination in the last chapter. Once more he defies all limits by requesting the celebration in spite of Rohan's death and by addressing Lucretia as his bride. Asking her to give him back his lost "young, fresh soul" (*W,* 265), he exhibits complete disregard for time and its order to which she has always strictly adhered. Savoring power and life he is encircled by death stemming from the recent enmity of the powerful Serbelloni and from an old, archaic feudal hatred, represented by Lucretia's servant Lucas. Unable to save Jürg from hired murderers and her servant, Lucretia slays him herself, suddenly claiming what she considers her exclusive right to take or not to take direct revenge on Jenatsch. Gottfried Keller's dissatisfaction with this finale[9] is understandable, since Lucretia's adherence to the revenge concept lacks convincing motivation. David Jackson, however, rightly suggests that, taken within the larger context of Jenatsch's life, this "perverted love-death"[10] is a necessary end to his destructive actions; and we might add that it seems a logical end to an existence based — as it was in the last part — on an inversion of values. While this end is wanting in psychological cogency it does conform to the action's deeply disturbing development.

The reaction of Chur's politicians to Jenatsch's assassination is typical of their ambivalent feelings toward him. By not prosecuting his murderers "who appeared to them as tools of a necessary fate" (*W,* 268) they show their relief at the death of this inordinate figure. At the same time, they lament him as "Graubünden's greatest man" and honor him with a pompous funeral. Thus, to the very end, Meyer keeps Jenatsch in an ambiguous light, refusing to give the reader a clear indication of whether heroic patriotism or selfish opportunism ultimately prevails. Given the complexity of the case and the limitations of the observers Waser and Sprecher, an attempt to come to terms with Jenatsch must lead to a sinuous argument: In Chapter 14 Waser's initial assumption that Jürg's "overwhelming patriotism" represents "the *one* aspect [in which] Georg Jenatsch surpasses our greatest contemporaries" is immediately modified: "I must admit that he has sacrificed more to it than a straight conscience can account for. But . . . is it not fortunate for us honorable statesmen if, for the good of the country, necessary deeds which cannot be executed by pure hands are taken over by such lawless men of violence — whom the omniscient god in His justice may judge. For they, too, are His instruments . . ." (*W,* 251). Sprecher, the historian, rejects such a casuistic argument: "This is a strangely dangerous tenet. . . . This is the direct way to justifying the worst crimes." But some casuistry is present in his view too: "Consider how easily such a lawless and unprincipled man, once thrown into his erratic path . . . may destroy his own successful work" (*W,* 251–52). Implicitly, Sprecher acknowledges the value of Jenatsch's work. More disturbing than the two men's inability to take an unambiguous stand is the self-righteousness which colors their thinking. The work's conclusion is thus as limited as the characters making it.

Since Meyer never speaks in his own name and since he did not create a truly respectable arbiter, his personal — ultimately negative — opinion is only indicated in such indirect ways as the substantiation of Grimani's fears, the increase in negative acts on Jürg's side, the emergence of his hubris, and his assassination. With this indirect procedure, Meyer pursues several objectives. By exposing the reader to different interpretations which are all, to some extent, plausible he wants to illustrate how difficult a clear judgment actually is in such a complex case. This difficulty is rooted in the contradictory development of events — Jenatsch's betrayal achieves freedom, Rohan's integrity is ineffective — and in the fact that Jenatsch's actions result not only from his individual temperament but also — as is shown most clearly in his copying Richelieu's methods — from his environment full of fanaticism and power politics. This view of the individual as at least a partial product of his time bears the mark of modern thinking transcending any rigid bourgeois morality. Despite an undeniable fascination with greatness Meyer is already removed from idealizing heroism in the manner typical for the middle class in the later nineteenth century.

Careful examination of the work reveals a basic pessimism similar to that of the Swiss historian Jacob Burckhardt, who was convinced that power in itself was evil. Such a suspicion of power, however, was in the 1870s an unpopular view, especially in Germany where Bismarck had just given successful examples of using all the power available in the name of patriotism. Bismarck and his *Realpolitik*—based on power rather than on ideas—constituted the contemporary phenomenon with which Meyer wanted to take issue. On September 26, 1886, he wrote to Haessel with regard to the Jenatsch material: "Moreover, it is remarkable that that period ... gives rise to, even necessitates a discussion of the same questions which agitate the world: I mean the conflict between right and might, politics and ethics" (*B*, II, 13). as in the case of *Hutten,* Meyer felt compelled to disguise his scruples, but additional writing experience and the context of a larger prose work provided him with more versatility and the wide scope necessary for an extensive use of irony. In a thorough study Valentin Herzog shows that a variety of ironic techniques permeate the entire work. Major and minor characters are combined in such ways as to point up contrasts and parallels which function as ironic restrictions for the main figures — ironically, the easy-going Fausch is more principled in religious matters than Jenatsch, and Rohan's lack of insight into human nature is ironically accentuated by his distrust of the perspicacious contradictions in symbols, views, and events, Meyer, according to Herzog, preserves distance and presents everything as relative.[11]

The frequent change in point of view is characteristic of Meyer's style which is one of stark contrasts and rapid changes — more a style of montage than of progressive development. This is obvious in his rigorously condensing the action of eighteen years into three short periods while leaving large intervals completely unaccounted for. In his stimulating analysis of Meyer's handling of time in *Jenatsch,* Günther Müller concludes that such temporal selectivity

— of 6570 days only fourteen are singled out for detailed description — substantially contributes to presenting the protagonist as a monumental figure.[12] Abruptness also marks the descriptions of the changes in Jürg's attitude: his betrayal and conversion are shown as sudden turnabouts. In the case of the conversion the scarcity of explanation is even more striking when we consider that, in response to criticism of that very fact, Meyer added a new chapter (now Chapter 12) to the book edition of 1876. Yet he still passes over the conversion, touching only briefly on its political advantage.

These narrative traits have a bearing not only on Meyer's style, but on the question of the literary genre of *Jürg Jenatsch*. In his letters, Meyer refers to it as "novel" and "novella," but its subtitle simply reads "A Story of Bünden," thus indicating the author's own uncertainty with regard to the work's generic character. As two recent studies indicate, Meyer scholars continue to disagree on this point. W. D. Williams excludes *Jenatsch* as a matter of course from his book *The Stories of C. F. Meyer* (1962) in which he discusses Meyer in the framework of the novella; by the same token, Georges Brunet includes *Jenatsch* without hesitation in his equally novella-oriented study *C. F. Meyer et la nouvelle* (1967). Except for its length, the work has clear affinities with the novella, since it focuses so exclusively on Jenatsch and on the dramatic climaxes of his story, there being neither gradual developments nor subplots. A letter to A. Meissner of March 1, 1875, shows that Meyer at times must have thought along these lines: "Jenatsch is definitely not a novel, rather I would call it a novella. At least, if the novel is of a more epic and the novella of a more dramatic character" (*B*, II, 265).

III   Der Schuss von der Kanzel

The basis for this style of contrasts is formulated in Meyer's next work, the short novella *Der Schuss von der Kanzel* (*The Shot from the Pulpit,* 1878). It is a by-product of *Jenatsch,* since its leading character is Rudolf Wertmüller now some thirty-five years older and himself a successful general in the service of the Austrian emperor. Endowed with Meyer's lifelong predilection for the *Odyssee* Wertmüller praises the work in Chapter 4 with the words: "Pfannenstiel, you have felt that the second part of the Odyssee is of particular beauty and greatness. How? At his own hearth, the

returning wanderer is mistreated as a vagrant beggar. How? The
suitors persuade themselves that he will never return, and yet they
sense his presence. They are laughing, and their faces are already
distorted by the convulsions of death — this is poetry" (*W,* XI,
89–90). Contrasts, sudden shifts from one extreme to another, and
ambivalence constitute the essence of poetic writing, because they
allow for the dramatic effects and the intensity of feeling that, for
Meyer, distinguish poetic creations from everyday life. Contractions thus mark his style on every level — in his sporadic handling
of time and action, centering on only a few features in the portrayal
of characters, in composing ambivalent images and symbols. The
most obvious form of such contractions occurs in the paradoxical
titles which he uses repeatedly: *Der Schuss von der Kanzel; Plautus
im Nonnenkloster (Plautus in the Nunnery); Die Hochzeit des
Mönchs (The Monk's Wedding); Angela Borgia.*

Though set against a somber background of war and death
reminiscent of *Jenatsch,* this new novella seems, at first, totally different, exhibiting a gift of humor in Meyer and presenting life in an
idyllic light. The story culminates in the comic event, the shot from
the pulpit, after which General Wertmüller, the eccentric but good-
hearted stage manager, sets things straight in the small world of
Mythikon: he unites the lovers — the naive minister Pfannenstiel
and Rahel Wertmüller, the daughter of Mythikon's patrician minister, and settles them in the modest world of Mythikon's parsonage.
He settles Rahel's father, his cousin, who scandalizes his flock with
his passion for hunting, in a more congenial capacity as game-
keeper on one of his properties; and he bequeathes to the Mythi-
konians a piece of land which, to their annoyance, intersects their
commons. Scholars have attributed the serenity of the work to
Meyer's new sense of contentment resulting from his marriage and
his acquisition of his home in Kilchberg.[13] While this is, to some
extent, true, one should not overlook the negative implications of
the idyll. The fictitious name Mythikon contains an element of
unreality which is heightened by the fact that all other places in the
story bear the real names of a setting very familiar to Meyer,
namely, that of Lake Zurich and of the peninsula Au, the place of
his engagement to Luise Ziegler. The comic characters — the
comfort-loving minister Rosenstock, the sentimental Pfannenstiel,
the parsimonious, self-righteous Krachhalder — are so limited in
vision that they see the unorthodox general as a sort of devil. In
contrast to the general's wide experience, to his world full of classi-

cal allusions, the bourgeois existence in its complacency and prejudice is shown as severely constricted. The idyll exists at the cost of
ıny participation in a more significant world, and the author's
sympathies clearly lie with the general who escaped his small native
world both physically and mentally. Using the comic to express his
deep dissatisfaction with the narrow-mindedness of his immediate
surroundings, Meyer tinges the light surface of the work with a
more acrid element.

With regard to this work, which he had written at the insistence
of his friend J. R. Rahn, Meyer had ambiguous, even negative feelings. In a letter to Wille of August 8, 1877, he called it "absurd
stuff which really does not suit me" (*W*, IX, 250); and on December 14 he confessed to Wille: "To me personally the comic always
leaves a bitter taste while the tragic elevates and edifies me"
(*B*, I, 160). Alfred Zäch explains this aversion to the comic in general and to his own comic gift with Meyer's upbringing in a Pietist
atmosphere where easy enjoyment of life was cause for a bad conscience.[14] Applying psychoanalytical insights, Lee B. Jennings
interprets the author's discomfort as stemming "from the fact that
his own inner tensions, being offered no opportunity of sublima-
tion in this 'lowly' genre, threaten to expose themselves."[15] In discussing Pfannenstiel's dream of the enticing Turkish woman, the
death symbols surrounding the masculine Wertmüller, and the pis-
tol shot — a symbol of virility — in such an inappropriate place as
a church, Jennings makes a case for his theory that Meyer here
alludes to erotic matters which, for him as well as Pfannenstiel,
carry negative implications of inappropriateness, danger, and even
punishment. But Meyer succeeds in enriching the story with
inventive comic points and droll names — Pfannenstiel ("pan-
handle") comically contrasts with the young man's sense for poetry
while Rosenstock ("rose plant") has a completely prosaic nature.
The denouement, however, is somewhat contrived and even borders on the painful so that it fails to gratify the reader with a fully
liberating laughter. This and Meyer's discomfort with the comic are
signs that not even at this point of artistic success and social
rehabilitation could he feel truly at one with a spontaneous unreflected existence.

CHAPTER 5

The Veil of Form

W ITH the novella *Der Heilige* (*The Saint*) Meyer turned to the
Middle Ages, to Thomas Becket, chancellor of King Henry II
of England and later archbishop of Canterbury, who was murdered
in Canterbury's cathedral in 1170 and canonized two years later.
Since the 1850s Meyer had been familiar with Becket's story and
with its account in Thierry's *Histoire de la conquête de l'Angle-
terre,* which was his main source for the work.[1] A first version of a
novella about Thomas Becket, entitled *Der neue Heilige,* was
apparently completed in 1875,[2] but then abandoned until 1877. Yet
almost two years of intensive work were necessary to finish this
novella which increasingly fascinated its author. Nearing the end,
Meyer wrote to Gottfried Kinkel on March 16, 1879: "I must hurry
or else *The Saint* will make me lose what little is left of my religion"
(*W,* 287). And to Julius Rodenberg, who published the novella in
his *Deutsche Rundschau* (1879–1880) he admitted in a letter of May
6 that he had become particularly attached to the work "because of
the more psychic than intellectual exertion that it required"
(*W,* 287).

Becket's story captivated Meyer's imagination. As chancellor,
Thomas was a shrewd politician and an elegant, haughty courtier
enjoying all the privileges of the Norman aristocracy despite his low
Saxon birth. After having been appointed archbishop through the
will of the king, he suddenly turned into a bare-footed ascetic — a
protector of the downtrodden Saxons — and into an austere martyr. Was this astounding change the result of a true conversion or
rather of some hidden cunning? With his nineteenth-century skepticism Meyer was deeply attracted by this potential ambivalence and
used it as the basis for his unorthodox interpretation of the medieval saint.

For this end he significantly altered the historical material. First, he embroiders Thierry's report that Becket's mother was of Saracen origin (see the poem "Mit zwei Worten" — "With Two Words") and lets the young Becket spend a happy time in Cordova in Moorish Spain. Second, he deviates completely from the sources by having Becket marry the Cordovan Calif's sister who dies giving birth to their first child Grazia. While this is related in the form of a fairy tale about "Prince Moonbeam" and "Princess Sun" (*W,* 22–23), the course of the story clearly identifies "Prince Moonbeam" as Becket. Back in England Becket keeps the existence of his adored daughter secret. But one day the barely grown-up girl is discovered and seduced by King Henry, and a few months later she is killed in an abduction attempt. Becket is wounded to the depths of his soul. Therefore, his historical conduct as archbishop — opposing the power of the crown — could be seen, under the guise of evangelical commitment, as a most sublime form of personal revenge against the king. In other words, Meyer underplays Becket's historical martyrdom with an unhistorical personal problem. He tries to explain the phenomenon of this medieval saint by means of psychological and purely human reactions, thus creating a figure that vacillates enigmatically between saintly devotion and worldly vindictiveness. Or, as the author himself expressed it in a letter of May 2, 1880, to Lingg: "In the act of his conversion revengefulness and piety interpenetrate in an uncanny manner" (*W,* 299). In other letters, Meyer also insists that *Der Heilige* is "intentionally ambiguous" (*W,* 300) and that it is a composition that is "ambiguous like life itself" (*W,* 287).

While *Der Heilige* constitutes another, even sharper formulation of Meyer's technique of ambiguity, the work differs from the preceding novellas in its new accent on form. Here for the first time Meyer uses a frame which is interwoven with the actual story in such a way that the narrative presentation, interspersed with doubting questions by a listener, becomes an integral part of the story's meaning. The frame introduces a narrator, a Swiss crossbow maker named Hans der Armbruster who, in his capacity as a personal servant to King Henry, is a direct eyewitness to many crucial conversations and events in the dramatic relationship between the king and his chancellor and archbishop. Thus, Hans' own life story guarantees the reality of the tale that he is recounting to his acquaintance, Canon Burkhard, in Zurich twenty-one years after Becket's death, in — as Meyer wrote to Betty Paoli — an "idyllic" environment far

removed from "the bitter and cruel story" (*W,* 296). Burkhard
represents religious orthodoxy and political conservatism, and as a
monarchist he sides with the king. Repeatedly, he interrupts and
questions Hans, whose account of the events offends his strict
views. Burkhard's sense of order is disturbed because this supposed
"saint" opposes a Christian — not a pagan — king and because, in
Chapter 10, Hans disregards the actual chronicle dates which seem
to him to be "empty figures" (*W,* 105) when compared with the
ultimate significance of events and characters seen from a distance
and in a larger context. And although Hans has a quick mind and
has seen many countries, including pagan Spain, his view of Becket
is nevertheless limited by his servant position and the inescapable
conventions of medieval thinking. Thus, the framework functions
in a multiple way: it establishes Hans' report as a close-up view, as
the privileged view of an eyewitness; and while it stresses narrow-
mindedness in Burkhard, it also points up the narrator's own
limitations in understanding. In Meyer's words, "Hans only [com-
prehends] the external side of the story" (*W,* 297). Therefore,
tangible objects and events assume special significance.

In *Der Heilige* Meyer successfully carries out his conviction that
in poetic creation the abstract must be made concrete.[3] He achieves
a new mastery in presenting abstract concepts by means of visual
images, colorful characters, telling actions, and incidents. A wealth
of detail and a host of secondary characters provide a diverse and
lively background. But every detail functions in reference to the
central character. The concretization reaches an extreme in
Becket's daughter Grace, whom Walter Silz criticizes as "colorless
and unconvincing . . . [she] remains a symbol and an abstrac-
tion. . . ."[4] This assessment is not completely unjustified, yet the
figure of Grace must be seen in the light of Meyer's intentions.
First, she is not meant to be a full-blooded young woman but symbolizes an untouched, pure existence that has not yet entered full
life. As Mary C. Chrichton shows,[5] she resembles the virgin Eve
emerging as a still pure idea from God's creation in the poem "Die
Jungfrau" ("The Virgin"). Second, Grace's function — as well as
that of the entire episode involving her — indicates that, with all
the vividness present in the work, Meyer's first goal was not so
much realism but the capturing of enigmatic life in aesthetic form.

Form, however, is not only important in a structural way but also
as an integral part of Becket's existence and behavior. Becket is a
man of form: although he is the son of a common Saxon merchant

he has become the model courtier whose refinement — described in Chapter 4 — is admired by the Norman aristocrats as "the ultimate in courtly perfection" (*W,* 37). Combining engaging form with an ingenious mind, he is an excellent diplomat. Of low birth and delicate disposition, he depends on fashionable elegance and intellectual superiority to gain respect and influence among the Norman aristocracy holding the raw power. Meyer attributes these talents to Becket's Saracen heritage and his stay in Moorish Spain. The "pagan" Arab culture comes to symbolize a world of superior thinking — Hans praises the Spaniards' knowledge in mathematics, and mechanics (*W,* 22) — and of refined form, as shown in their elaborate architecture.

In this world Becket feels most at home; the fairy tale about Prince Moonbeam suggests that here he found deep, almost paradisiac fulfillment though only for a short time. Despite certain imperfections — Princess Sun dies, the calif resorts to repulsive, bloody political means — Spain remains for Becket a world of delicate beauty and peace. This gratifying experience belongs, according to Mary C. Crichton, to his innermost soul and is symbolized in Grace as well as in the atmosphere associated with, and created for, her. In England, she lives in a secluded castle in Moorish style, the game grazes freely around it, and in Chapter 5 Becket himself, having discarded his "coldly scrutinizing look," resembles a "pious knight or pilgrim to the Holy Grail," his face shows a "blissful kindness," and his purple gown suggests a priestly garment (*W,* 49). The essence of this world is reflected in the girl's name, Grace, which oscillates between grace denoting "the finest flower of human nature and charm" (*W,* 59) and divine grace reminiscent of Becket's converted Saracen mother, who was rechristened Grace. This name, as well as the comparison of Becket with a knight of the Grail indicates that his contact with a "pagan" culture does not exclude all Christian belief. But because of cultural refinement it does exclude the conventional medieval religion with its polarization of Christian and pagan, God and devil as exemplified in the episode of the witch Black Mary. Becket's psychological understanding of Mary's case appears as heresy in light of the death verdict which the king, in his capacity as "[being] the Christian conscience of England" (*W,* 39), considers it his highest duty to pronounce.

In sum, Becket is an outsider in England, a man of modern psychological, relativistic thinking in an absolutistic time, an aesthete, a priest of form and nuances in a world of crude concepts, battles, and unreflected existence. This latter is chiefly represented by the king, who loves wild hunting and indulges unrestrainedly in every emotion — a man "of changing moods like April, harsh, impatient, irascible, terrible in anger, but then again of an effusive disposition, affable and cordial..." (W, 34). And while Henry typifies the man of naive, ebullient force, the Norman barons exhibit only the negative side of such an existence. They are mainly interested in power and are all too ready to pander to the destructive desires of their royal master. For example, Gui Malherbe, an impudent seducer of Saxon girls, is instrumental in carrying out the queen's desire to have Grace killed, and four Norman barons quickly execute Henry's wish to be rid of Becket. In this world of crude emotions Grace cannot survive, and with her destruction Becket's innermost life, his last belief in harmony, is shattered. In Chapter 6, the scene in the chapel where Grace lies in state shows beauty without life, and Becket's own face is "more lifeless and more dead than that of the corpse" (W, 64). When Hans reminds him of the king, deep hatred burns in his eyes like "a flame, cruel and full of bitter grief like hell" (W, 65). But soon he seems to go about his duties as chancellor with the same formal mastery as before — albeit for some changes. In the middle of a banquet his face appears dead, he becomes more Christian and alleviates, though timidly, the Saxons' lot. He ardently addresses a roughly hewn crucifix, though in Arabic and with expressions of implacable grief and, in Hans' view, almost blasphemous doubts. Inwardly dead, his ideal cruelly broken, he now feels more in tune with a world of suffering and imperfect forms.

The king continues to trust his chancellor. In his one-dimensional thinking he relies on the admitted flaw of Becket's Oriental nature, his subservience to power, and overlooks the other Oriental element, his vindictiveness. Therefore, he cannot fathom the threatening implication of Becket's warning in Chapter 7: "Never give me up to a master who would be more powerful than yourself! ... For in the ignominy of my meekness I would have to obey him in every way and to execute his commands even against you, oh king of England..." (W, 75). The king knows of only one power — the political one — and thus his plan to appoint Becket archbishop is conceived only as a political move by which the pagan unbeliever would fulfill the king's desire to have the jurisdiction of church and clergy curtailed. Despite his ambition and his opposition to the official church Becket demurs. Superior in intellect but inferior in social position he had long ago developed subtle ways of thinking and a deeply ironic attitude. Thus he recognizes the potential irony of the scheme offered to him: it is an intrinsic irony (*Ironie der Sache*) that the primacy, understood in a really spiritual way, might jeopardize Henry's power rather than expand it. Furthermore, it is the irony of the situation that Becket, behind the forms of perfect politeness and loyalty to the king, might feel critical enough to use the primacy against the crown, or might even be susceptible to one of "those sudden changes that may come upon a man who changes his clothes and dons clerical garb" (*W*, 85).

The question whether or not Becket, forced to take on the new role, becomes an exemplary Christian bishop can only be judged by external signs; thus, it is Meyer's use of form that gives it all its enigmatic fascination. Once again, Becket proves to be a stunning master of form. Overnight he changes from an aesthete into an ascetic, emphatically disdaining all the customary pomp accorded high ecclesiastical dignitaries, embracing instead evangelical poverty and the causes of the poor, downtrodden Saxons. Although he immerses himself in the religion of the land he is again an outsider in the environment of the church. The very quickness of the change casts suspicion on this new form which Henry, in Chapter 9, first tries to dismiss as nothing but an astute lesson in "true apostolic behavior" (*W*, 88) administered to the other bishops. But Becket's discarding of worldly riches and honors is deeply rooted in his acute sense of inner deprivation since Grace's death; thus he can say to Henry: "I am no different from what I appear to be" (*W*, 94). This Christian conduct also transcends the purely individual sphere resulting in real political demands and bringing Becket into perilous opposition to king and clergy. In anticipation of a violent death, Becket's behavior becomes more and more an *imitatio Christi* in words, gestures, and — most poignantly — in his silent defiance of the four murderers. The Christian form, thus, seems substantiated by suffering and death.

This form, however, is interspersed with disturbing remnants of Becket's old aesthetic and worldly attitudes. In a last attempt of reconciliation he refuses the king the kiss of peace. By emphasizing the mixture of "ugliness and desire" (*W*, 118) in Hery's face Meyer indicates that Becket reacts as an aesthete and as humanly vindictive, thus displaying attitudes which run counter to evangelical principles. Implacable rigor seems involved in another crucial refusal, that of declining the king's protection — offered through Hans — against the murderers. Other elements support this motive of suicidal revenge, too. Before the attempted reconciliation in Chapter 11 Meyer briefly introduces the troubador and political satirist Bertran de Born who greets the exiled Becket as a brother in hate: "You suffer as did your master, and you will let yourself be killed as he did ... and your death, like that of your God, will be the damnation of men!" (*W*, 111). In a much subtler way, the smile on Becket's dying face could reflect the satisfaction of personal revenge and the ultimate triumph of the weak over the powerful in the sense of Becket's philosophy outlined in Chapter 4: "I am fond of thinking and art, and I like it ... when the weaker one hits and conquers the stronger one from a distance" (*W*, 33).

In Becket's motivation, Meyer intends to intertwine the extremes of exemplary faithfulness and implacable revenge in order to emphasize the strange, ironic coincidence of personal motives with larger, uncontrollable forces such as the king's command and what seems to be God's will. Grace's death not only engenders deep hate and a feeling of internal deprivation, but also intensifies Becket's older disdain for Henry and the "miasma" of his court, "where nothing pure can prosper" (*W*, 58). In addition, it sharpens his aversion to the means he has to use in politics and by which "the empires of this world are governed," such as "violence, bribery, betrayal" (*W*, 86). The primacy unexpectedly offers him a perfect form in which to express his feelings of disgust toward the world in which he is living. More importantly, it provides him with the framework for associating his negative judgment of Henry with God's will, for giving his individual opinion a divine sanction. As archbishop, Becket considers himself a direct instrument for the divine punishment of Henry; when the murderers ask him from whom he had received the power of his see he answers, conscious of the terrible irony: "From the hands of my king for his judgment!" (*W*, 132).

The criticism about *Der Heilige* understandably mirrors the work's complex nature that allows for varying interpretations. One group of scholars aims at determining whether true piety or sublime hate ultimately motivate Becket's actions. Robert d'Harcourt (1913), Harry Maync (1925), and W. E. Yuill (1961), for example, see revenge as the essential motive, while George Brunet (1967) holds that the saint's aureole clearly prevails over the diabolical possibility. W. A. Coupe (1962) considers Becket's role in the destruction of Henry as "an entirely passive one" and thus views Becket as a true instrument of God's punishment of Henry.[6] Robert Faesi (1924), W. D. Williams (1962), Colin Walker (1968), and Lewis W. Tusken (1971) stress Becket's ultimately impenetrable ambivalence and surmise that both his revenge and his Christian devotion are largely real. Walker and Tusken especially try to analyze this ambiguity in greater detail. Walker avers that Becket becomes increasingly Christ-like, but that by refusing the king's protection he insists on becoming a martyr. This entails his determination that "the guilt of the murder should be on Henry's head" as a fitting punishment.[7] Walker therefore concludes that Becket's revenge lies less in his conduct as archbishop than in his death in which he usurps, in an unsaintly manner, the vengeance that should be God's. Lewis W. Tusken also emphasizes a fusion of "mortal egotism and divine will" in Becket's actions, but from it he infers that Meyer deliberately oversimplified the medieval concept of divine justice so as to show, by means of irony, that divine reason cannot be completely analyzed.[8] While these studies elucidate the complicated nature of the story to some extent, they also show that Becket's existence cannot be completely unraveled. The very plurality of plausible interpretations shows how successful Meyer was in creating an ambiguity that, in his own words, was an intention (see *W*, 300) as well as an inspiration — "I wrote the 'Saint' almost unconsciously, obsessed, in an intoxicated state.... But I *had* to write it as I did" (*W*, 301).

Far from being a weak afterthought, as Coupe suggests, ambiguity is of crucial importance in this work. On the intellectual level, it is designed to emphasize Meyer's conviction that the conventional concepts of "saint" and "faith" are incommensurate with a reality that proves to be complex. On the level of personal, psychological motivation it makes allowance for the modern insight that phenomena such as sanctity may be bound up with reactions that are purely human and not, first and foremost, of an absolute, religious nature. In this respect Meyer is quite close to Nietzsche who, in the chapter "Das religiöse Leben" in *Menschliches Allzumenschliches (Human All Too Human),* dissects the phenomena of Christian asceticism and religion into a series of subtle fancies masking egotism with piety and higher religious commands.[9] Of course, the unbeliever Nietzsche is far more scathing in his analysis than the cautious, ambivalent Meyer could ever be. Despite this difference in temperament, Meyer exhibits the same modern way of scrutinizing the miraculous conversion from a psy-chological-relativistic standpoint. To be sure, he leaves the question open and the reader's judgment free, but by creating such an indestructible link between revenge and sanctity he strikes out in a new direction for which many of his contemporary readers were not ready. Especially in Switzerland the reception of the work was marred by misjudgments stemming from a narrow-minded, puritan reaction to the rape of Grace; it was said that the book could not be put into a woman's hands (*W,* 291). To what extent Meyer felt mis-understood can be measured by the fact that, contrary to his cus-tom, he repeatedly and extensively commented on the work (*W,* 296–301). Not until the twentieth century did *Der Heilige* acquire the reputation of being one of Meyer's finest works — per-haps his finest.

Finally, this novella is ambiguous on the level of form, too. As has been pointed out, the framework constitutes an interplay between objective facts and subjectively limited points of view. Hans' report furnishes a close view of the controversial saint, but Becket's thoughts and actual intentions remain inaccessible. Thus the story is presented as a close-up view but lacks its clarity; and consequently, the narrative form is revealing and concealing at the same time. The same is true with respect to the modes of Becket's behavior: certainly, they are suggestive, and for the reader they reveal more than Hans is aware of, but they never really unveil Becket's innermost life. With all its expressiveness, form here does not disclose all its content. This use of form as a veil is part of Meyer's relativistic attitude, of his distrust of all absolute claims at a time of growing awareness of the complexities in human motiva-tion. Using form in this way allows Meyer to leave the question open, to suggest a modern, psychological interpretation of religious phenomena without having completely to reject the traditional views. For Meyer, the veil of form was a necessity if he was to suc-ceed in expressing personal thoughts at variance with the conven-tions of the seemingly well-ordered bourgeois world around him.

CHAPTER 6

Flaming Signals on Dark Waters: Meyer's Poetry

F OR all his extensive work in prose since 1872, Meyer was far from neglecting his poetry which, for long, had been his prime endeavor. And it is in poetry that, after an arduous working process, he was to reach his most innovative accomplishments. Letters and manuscripts of the 1870s reveal continuous work on poems which were published individually or in small groups in several poetry journals. For years, Meyer and Haessel could not agree on the terms for a poetry collection which Meyer had proposed as early as 1873 (*W,* II, 8–10). Thus, the preparation of such a collection — simply entitled *Gedichte (Poems)* — in 1881–1882 meant for him the realization of a cherished plan.

With utmost care Meyer reviewed all his poems written before 1881, many of which had already been revised several times. Among those chosen for the collection there is scarcely one that was not altered, at least in some minor way, and almost half of them were recast into a *Neufassung* differing from the preceding version in meter, length, and at times even in crucial imagery.[1] The *Gedichte* of 1882 thus represent a sort of poetic *summa,* the result of Meyer's unique effort of patient revising and experimenting. Spanning two decades, this effort proceeds from mediocre beginnings to original poems, from wordy, long-winded narrative poems to concise, dramatic ballads, from conventional lyrics to delicately wrought images and to symbolist poems unfolding new poetic possibilities and, in some cases, highest perfection. Thanks to Betsy, this whole process can be closely traced in the hundreds of manuscripts which, over the long years of her collaboration, she had set aside one by one as soon as they had become obsolete. Thus

95

she saved this material from certain destruction by Meyer himself, who was not at all interested in work which he had already surpassed.[2] The entire manuscript material is being published by Hans Zeller in the critical Meyer edition: Volumes 2–5 will contain the material relating to the *Gedichte,* Volumes 6 and 7 the collections *Zwanzig Balladen von einem Schweizer* (*Twenty Ballads by a Swiss,* 1864) and *Romanzen und Bilder* (*Ballads and Images,* 1869) as well as the material relating to all other poems. Thus, Zeller's edition will offer an unusual opportunity for observing a poet at work.

I   *Toward a New Lyricism*

To be sure, Meyer is not the only poet who diligently reworked his poems. Yet his travail is singular in the persistence he applied to a relatively small body of poems which, at that, contains an even smaller number of concepts and motifs. In the course of rewriting, Meyer often achieves astonishing results by refining images, by slowly unveiling the full depths of symbols, by isolating, developing, and interchanging motifs. One motif often becomes the focus for several related yet still diverse poems, for example, Charon's boat for the so-called lake poems, namely, "Die toten Freunde" ("Dead Friends"), "Schwüle" ("Sultry Day"), "Eingelegte Ruder" ("Oars at Rest"), "Im Spätboot" ("Nocturnal Boat"); or the figure of the dead beloved for a group of love poems, "Weihgeschenk" ("Votive Offering"), "Der Blutstropfen" ("A Drop of Blood"), "Wetterleuchten" ("Heat Lightning"), "Lethe," "Stapfen" ("Footsteps"). Repeatedly, two or three different pieces derive from the same early poem, for example, the early versions of "Der tote Achill" ("Dead Achilles") are also the basis for "Der Gesang des Meeres" ("Song of the Sea") and "Möwenflug" ("Sea gulls in Flight"), and the poem "Der Triumphbogen" ("Triumphal Arch") uses an isolated motif from "Der Musensaal" ("Hall of the Muses"). In his fundamental study *The Poetry of Conrad Ferdinand Meyer,* Heinrich Henel characterizes this development as "proliferation" which, in an intriguing way, combines "organic growth and conscious manipulation."[3] Several charts exhibit the complexity of a creative process the strength of which lies less in imagining new motifs and symbols than in elaborating and interlinking the ones that his imagination had produced quite early — in the 1860s when he concentrated on poetry — but in embryonic form. Like Schiller, Meyer builds his poetic world with "a small family of concepts." Therefore, it is no surprise to find topics from ballads in the novellas, for example, "Der Mars von Florenz" ("Mars of Florence") in *Die Hochzeit des Mönchs,* "Mit zwei Worten" ("With Two Words") in *Der Heilige,* "Cäsar Borgias Ohnmacht" ("Cesar Borgia Powerless") in *Angela Borgia,* and to recognize many lyric motifs in the novellas.

Meyer's persistence in reworking his poems shows, more than anything else, how much importance he attached to his poetry. His comments, however, are quite contradictory. Only seldom does he speak positively about his poetic endeavors, so when he describes his lyric poems as "most delicate" (*W,* II, 28) and ventures the opinion that "on the whole, the collection holds — if I am not mistaken — its own" (*W,* II, 29). Much more often he takes a disparaging view, calling his poetry "sentimental," "not true enough," "rarely more than a play or, at the most, an expression of an inferior part of my nature" (*W,* II, 28-29). This ambivalence is rooted in his own uncertainty with regard to his poetry which he knew to be out of tune with the conventional lyric production of the time, and which, moreover, affords some rare — though still veiled — glimpses into his most personal experiences. Among the contemporary readers only a few — for instance, Gottfried Keller and Carl Spitteler — recognized the unusual beauty of Meyer's lyrics; most critics of the time preferred his historical ballads because they felt the lack of direct expression of emotions in the lyric poems. This opinion is summed up in Theodor Storm's words: ". . . for real lyric poetry he lacks the true 'tirili' of the soul. . . . [he lacks] the immediate, captivating expression of feeling, maybe even the immediate feeling itself" (*W,* II, 34). In the twentieth century, this assessment has been reversed, and the lyric poems are being appreciated as an important link in the emergence of symbolist poetry in German literature. Yet a comprehensive evaluation of both ballads and lyrics and their respective styles, their differences and similarities, is still lacking.

A look at German lyric poetry after 1860 makes us realize that the style created by Goethe and the romantics was still the prevalent model: the words "lyric" and "poetic" were tantamount to immediacy of feeling and expression, and a supple, melodious language. Reluctant, even unable, to bare his soul and with little talent for melodious verses Meyer was — as Storm rightly observes — ill suited for this kind of confessional poetry, or *Erlebnisdichtung.* Yet other models, though available in Goethe's nonconfessional objective poetry, or in Mörike's delicate epigrams, were overlooked and not recognized as such. In the many revisions of his poems Meyer, therefore, had to grope his way toward a style more akin to his own temperament. It was a slow, empirical process, and the results are varied in nature and, at times, uneven in quality but basically similar in their thrust toward a poetry in which immediacy is replaced by contemplation and objective description. The most striking achievement in this development are some consummate examples of symbolist poetry, a style which, rooted in German romanticism, first came into prominence in France in the work of Charles Baudelaire (1821–1869) and Stéphane Mallarmé (1842–1898) before it appeared in Germany in Stefan George's poetry in the 1890s and in Rainer Maria Rilke's *Neue Gedichte* in 1907–1908. In symbolism, the poet conveys his emotions indirectly in images which reveal subjective meaning mainly in their objective shape. The symbolist poet also stresses conscious composition over inspiration. In short, symbolism is antithetical to *Erlebnisdichtung* and, thus, an appropriate style for Meyer. Despite his interests in French literature, he had, however, no cognizance of Baudelaire or later symbolists;[4] in virtual isolation and without specific theoretical aims, he broke new ground in German poetry. From this stylistic point of view, Meyer's numerous revisions are most valuable documents because they allow us to trace the transition from romantic to symbolist poetry in the very particulars of creative work. Analyzing the entire development of individual poems is a rewarding task but too extensive for the limited space of this book, so that we have to refer the reader to the studies of Heinrich Henel, Emil Staiger, and other scholars.[5]

The decided focus on the outer world gives rise to two types of poems characteristic of Meyer's more modern poetry. Using the principle of analogy he likens the description of an external phenomenon to a trait of internal life. On the basis of detached contemplation ne provides a visual image with an invisible, sometimes emotional correspondence giving the poem a transparency unwonted at the time. One of the best examples for this type, which Henel calls *Gleichungsgedicht* ("poem of equation"),[6] is the short poem "Eppich" ("Ivy") whose structure perfectly mirrors the correlation of the two worlds in the two equal stanzas as well as in the rhetorical form of a dialogue between the poet and the ivy. While some of these poems, such as "Der verwundete Baum"

("The Injured Tree"), are somewhat contrived, felicitous poems like "Möwenflug" ("Sea gulls in Flight") and "Das Ende des Festes" ("The Banquet's End") show that the lucid correspondence between the two parts need not destroy the delicate veil of a poetic vision.

In another group of poems Meyer goes a step further: eliminating the explicit comparison he concentrates on describing an object, a visible image in such a way that the mere dispassionate description reveals the deeper symbolic meaning of the object. This so-called *Dinggedicht* ("object poem") finds a perfect example in "Der römische Brunnen" ("The Roman Fountain"), probably Meyer's best known poem:

> Aufsteigt der Strahl und fallend giesst
> Er voll der Marmorschale Rund,
> Die, sich verschleiernd, überfliesst
> In einer zweiten Schale Grund;
> Die zweite gibt, sie wird zu reich,
> Der dritten wallend ihre Flut,
> Und jede nimmt und gibt zugleich
>   Und strömt und ruht.

> Up rises the jet and falling
> Fills the marble bowl to its round rim,
> Which, veiling itself, flows over
> Into the depths of a second bowl;
> The second, becoming too rich, gives,
> Swelling up, its flood to the third,
> And each takes and gives at the same time
>   And flows and rests.

In this depiction, devoid of any comment or even an emotional tone, the reader recognizes the fountain as a symbol of life with its continuous flux and eternal permanence, as a living symbol of beauty with its balance between movement and rest, and a symbol of art that unites the all too often disparate elements of giving and taking. The image of the fountain with the water in endless cycle is delightful in its simplicity, which is, however, the result of much conscious work, as is evident from the poem's development through seven stages and twelve manuscripts (*W*, III, 242–49). Over the years this small work has generated numerous interpretations, among which is the recent one by Thomas E. Hart.[7] Analyzing the poem's language with the tools of precise linguistic description, Hart convincingly shows how sound patterns, metric and linguistic structures reflect the contrasts and parallels in imagery and meaning, how — in Hart's words — the poet "enlisted calculation to support inspiration." "Der römische Brunnen" is a poetic triumph representing, as it does, harmonious beauty in an immediately engaging, understandable image which, though elaborately wrought, preserves the simplicity of beauty that needs no explanation.

The poem "Zwei Segel" ("Two Sails") discloses another facet of the *Dinggedicht.* Meyer's subtle use of personalized words such as *empfinden, begehren, Gesell* impart an inner dimension to the otherwise wholly visual scene; thus the two boats following each other in unison come to symbolize love. The dominance of the external image makes it possible for Meyer to express inner, in some cases even personal feelings in a veiled, nonconfessional form. Thus the symbol in "Das Seelchen" ("Little Soul") contains an indication about his innermost self: using the classical symbol for the soul, the butterfly, he imagines it in a personal way when concluding with the lines: "Wie sind die Schwingen ihm gefärbt? / Sie leuchten blank, betupft mit Blut" ("How are his wings dyed? / They gleam brightly, flecked with blood"). The mottling of blood indicates the wounding of the unprotected, delicate soul. Other details hint at suffering as well: in contrast to the earth, the sky appears as "blissful blue," and the butterfly, ready to fly off, conveys the poet's — man's — yearning to leave a painful life.

Brevity and concentration on a single motif are characteristic of Meyer's symbolist poetry; they are the outward signs of an intrinsically different way of writing. In romantic poetry, symbols emerge from an experience in which the poet identifies his inner state with the external world, and such identification generates a number of symbols related to the experience and employed in one poem. In symbolist poetry, however, an external image, or a series of images is described in such ways that the depiction alone reveals the symbolic meaning that this object assumes for the poet with regard to life or to a personal experience.[8] The poet's basic attitude has changed from identification to contemplation. Like Hutten on the Ufenau, Meyer contemplates the world around him and his own experiences, and then carefully chooses individual external phenomena that lend themselves to being matched with and to express this or that internal feeling. In the poem "Liederseelen" ("Souls of

Songs"), which is reminiscent of the early Hutten poem "Der Zecher,"[9] Meyer outlines this procedure of seeing isolated motifs and of developing each one individually into a poem. And it is significant that the concluding lines give equal importance both to the inspiration and the poet's conscious selection: " 'Und die du wählst, und der's beschied / Die Gunst der Stunde, die wird ein Lied' " ("And the one you choose and the one destined / By a favorable hour becomes a song"). Thus "Liederseelen" constitutes — so to speak — Meyer's symbolist poetics *en miniature.* While the romantic group of symbols may encompass a wide world of feeling, these isolated motifs are more limited; even in their most elaborate form they express only the one aspect of the poet's world, of human emotions. Therefore, no one motif can express all of Meyer's world, and while some of them do have special weight, they still must be seen in the larger context of associated motifs. On the following pages, the main motifs will be discussed, starting with the ones relating to death and moving on to the motifs of the mountains, the harvest and Dionysian life, and continuing from there to the ballads.

II *Dark Waters: the Lake Poems*

Original in content and accomplished in form, Meyer's lake poems "Eingelegte Ruder," "Schwüle," "Im Spätboot," and "Nachtgeräusche" are among his finest lyric creations. With some variations they focus on the motif of a lonely boat on the lake at dusk or at night and on the dark and silent waters. Meyer's personal feeling of being close to death, his classical knowledge, and the familiar landscape coalesce in a quietly impressive image of weariness, ennui, and death. "Eingelegte Ruder" ("Oars at Rest") opens with an image which, in its lack of scenery and its dull calm, conveys the impression of total emptiness:

> Meine eingelegten Ruder triefen,
> Tropfen fallen langsam in die Tiefen.
>
> Nichts das mich verdross! Nichts das mich freute!
> Niederrinnt ein schmerzenloses Heute!
>
> Unter mir — ach, aus dem Licht verschwunden —
> Träumen schon die schönern meiner Stunden.
>
> Aus der blauen Tiefe ruft das Gestern:

Sind im Licht noch manche meiner Schwestern?

My locked oars drip,
Drops fall slowly to the depths.

Nothing pains me! Nothing gives me joy!
Down drips a painless today!

Beneath me — oh gone from the light —
My more beautiful hours are already dreaming.

From the blue depths yesterday calls:
Are many of my sisters still in the light?

This external emptiness of the first stanza corresponds to an internal one described in the following three stanzas. Nothing moves the poet, the present has no emotional content, no hold on him — like the drops of water from the oars it drips down without touching him. Whatever was worthwhile has long sunk to the depths of the lake. Nothing but the passing of time remains visible in the slowly falling drops, and this last trace of motion renders the calm even heavier. This leaden stillness is palpable in the form as well: the long trochaic line with its many long vowels is heavy and slow, and the simple rhyme couplets create a monotonous, falling cadence comparable to the falling drops. The weariness of life Meyer must have felt himself transcends the purely personal, because it is rooted in a deep disillusion with life that was newly growing in the nineteenth century and that Georg Büchner describes as *Langeweile* ("boredom") and Charles Baudelaire as ennui.

In "Schwüle" ("Sultry Day") the feeling of emptiness is given a more alarming dimension. In the face of a wan, hollow world, the call from the depths assumes a dreadful, yet alluring insistency which makes the need for even the faintest hope — the stars — desperately felt.

Trüb verglomm der schwüle Sommertag,
Dumpf und traurig tönt mein Ruderschlag —
Sterne, Sterne — Abend ist es ja —
Sterne, warum seid ihr noch nicht da?

Bleich das Leben! Bleich der Felsenhang!
Schilf, was flüsterst du so frech und bang?
Fern der Himmel und die Tiefe nah —
Sterne, warum seid ihr noch nicht da?

Eine liebe, liebe Stimme ruft
Mich beständig aus der Wassergruft —
Weg, Gespenst, das oft ich winken sah!
Sterne, Sterne, seid ihr nicht mehr da?

Endlich, endlich durch das Dunkel bricht —
Es war Zeit! — ein schwaches Flimmerlicht —
Denn ich wusste nicht wie mir geschah.
Sterne, Sterne, bleibt mir immer nah!

Gloomily the sultry summer day vanished,
Dull and sad the sound of my oars strikes —
Stars, stars — it is evening —
Stars, why are you not yet out?

Pale is life! Pale the rocky cliff!
Sedge, what is your brazen, frightened whisper?
Far the sky and the depths near —
Stars, why are you not yet out?

A dear, dear voice ceaselessly
Calls me from the watery grave —
Away, ghost, whom often I saw beckon!
Stars, stars, are you no longer there?

Finally, finally through the darkness breaks —
High time! — faint glimmering light —
For I did not know what was happening to me
Stars, stars, remain ever close to me!

For several reasons, the third stanza is of special significance. It contains a rarely occurring personal element by alluding to Meyer's mother, who drowned herself, and to his own occasional desire to end his life. The manuscripts reveal that this biographical reference was only added when Meyer revised the 1869 version in 1881–1882. Such a remark about the dark period of his life which he consistently passes over in silence is only possible when form and imagery for a poem are already established.[10] Nevertheless, this last touch proves to be the symbolic core of the poem. Only when the water is identified as the realm of death, the anxiety — caused by the empty sky, the livid landscape, the eerily rustling reeds, the close depths — is understandable in its full threat. Only now the repeated cry for the stars acquires its full significance as a dramatic emphasis of man's forlornness, his exposure to dark, destructive forces. The simple forms of rhyme and stanza as well as the many word repetitions, function as a sort of formal dam set up against the forces of

the depths that threaten to dissolve — as is evident in the chopped
sentences — all order and meaning of life.

 The full symbolism of the boat at night emerges in the poem "Im
Spätboot" ("Nocturnal Boat"):

> Aus der Schiffsbank mach ich meinen Pfühl,
> Endlich wird die heiße Stirne kühl!
> O wie süss erkaltet mir das Herz!
> O wie weich verstummen Lust und Schmerz!
> Ueber mir des Rohres schwarzer Rauch
> Wiegt und biegt sich in des Windes Hauch.
> Hüben hier und wieder drüben dort
> Hält das Boot an manchem kleinen Port:
> Bei der Schiffslaterne kargem Schein
> Steigt ein Schatten aus und niemand ein.
> Nur der Steurer noch, der wacht und steht!
> Nur der Wind, der mir im Haare weht!
> Schmerz und Lust erleiden sanften Tod:
> Einen Schlummrer trägt das dunkle Boot.

> On the ships' bench I rest my head,
> Finally my hot forehead cools!
> Oh how sweetly my heart grows cold!
> Oh how softly desire and pain grow silent!
> Above me, the black smoke from the stack
> Waves and bows to the wind's breath.
> Over here and then again over there
> The boat stops at several small ports:
> In the dim light of the ship's lantern
> A shadow climbs aboard, no one debarks.
> Only the helmsman, he still watches and stands!
> Only the wind which blows in my hair!
> Pain and desire suffer gentle death:
> The dark boat carries a slumberer.

As in "Die toten Freunde," Meyer is here bold enough to use the
modern steam boat — at the time considered unlyrical — for the
poem's setting. In his sparing description, the boat with her stead-
fast helmsman and the lone passenger turns into the symbol of
Charon's boat crossing from the shore of life to the land of the
dead. Death is shown as a barely perceptible passage: emotions are
dying down "sweetly" and "softly," resulting in an inner stillness
that is welcome as a long-awaited relief. Reality is fading away,
too: passengers leaving the boat and returning to reality appear as

mere shadows; death personified in the ever watchful helmsman is the only reality left. For even the poet's "I," present in the last traces of feelings at the beginning, even his consciousness is being effaced when, in the last line, he is referred to in the third person. With an everyday image and an almost prosaic language Meyer evokes a suggestive vision of death as a gentle passage into ultimate sleep and lasting peace.

A variation of this passage is found in "Nachtgeräusche" ("Night Sounds"):

> Melde mir die Nachtgeräusche, Muse,
> Die ans Ohr des Schlummerlosen fluten!
> Erst das traute Wachtgebell der Hunde,
> Dann der abgezählte Schlag der Stunde,
> Dann ein Fischer-Zwiegespräch am Ufer,
> Dann? Nichts weiter als der ungewisse
> Geisterlaut der ungebrochnen Stille,
> Wie das Atmen eines jungen Busens,
> Wie das Murmeln eines tiefen Brunnens,
> Wie das Schlagen eines dumpfen Ruders,
> Dann der ungehörte Tritt des Schlummers.·

> Announce the night sounds to me, Muse,
> Which lap at the ear of him who cannot sleep!
> First the familiar watchful bark of dogs,
> Then the strokes of the hour measured,
> Then two fishermen talking on the shore,
> Then? Nothing more than the uncertain
> Phantom sound of unbroken stillness,
> Like a young bosom's breathing,
> Like a deep well's murmuring,
> Like a muffled oar's beat,
> Then the unheard footfall of slumber.

Modest looking, this little poem is, on closer examination, a stunning poetic accomplishment. Focusing on familiar sounds audible at night and using the simplest form of enumeration, Meyer succeeds in creating a magic atmosphere of deepening silence. The sounds of dogs, clock, and fishermen are the last traces of wonted daily life. The third suspended "Dann" marks the point where silence becomes prevalent in the outside world. Yet Meyer penetrates this silence by noting another series of sounds echoing an internal realm of unfathomable depths. The "stroke of a muffled oar'' at the end suggests the beat of a pulse, a sound of life that is even more internal than that of breathing mentioned before. Together with the stroke of the clock, this beat points to the outer and inner world, to outer and inner time. And finally, the idea of the ''muffled oar'' is reminiscent of Charon's boat; thus the approaching sleep can also be understood as death.

Here, to an even greater extent than in "Spätboot," Meyer expands the realm of the expressible to the very limits of consciousness. He does this with seemingly simple means. The motif of the external sounds is quite plain, only the invocation of the muse is openly poetic. The language is simple, too: with the exception of one enjambment (lines 6–7) each syntactical unit fills a line. As in "Eingelegte Ruder" and "Spätboot," Meyer uses the trochaic pentameter, which here, however, is rhymeless except for one rhyme (lines 4–5). In conjunction with the prevailing *u* assonances, this rhyme provides a certain melodious quality. Only once the *u* sounds are interrupted by an *i* assonance (lines 6–7) at the point where the silence itself becomes audible. Moreover, the suspended ''Dann?'' and the following enjambment create the impression that the silence is expanding until, in the last line, it pervades everything.

III   *Death and Distance: The Love Poems*

These lake poems clearly demonstrate how far Meyer had departed from romantic poetry. Night, for the romantics, was a realm filled with intense yearning and promise, suggestive of a wide, enticing world; for Meyer, night has become almost void, a realm open only toward the depths, promising only peace in sleep or death. And while romantic poets follow rushing streams while fascinated by the mysteries of ever changing life, Meyer focuses on the stagnating waters of a lake while attracted by death. The significance which death has for Meyer separates him from the romantics in yet another way: in a group of beautiful love poems he sees the beloved as a young girl who died years ago unfulfilled. Love, since Goethe the epitome of immediate lyric expression, is presented not only in retrospect but also transfixed by death. Earlier scholars, especially Lena F. Dahme, established biographical connections between this ''junggebliebne Tote'' (''eternally youthful dead'') in the poems and two young women who briefly played a role in Meyer's emotional life: Constance von Rodt (1839–1858) whom he knew in 1853, and Clelia Weydmann (1837–1866) whom he admired in 1860. But neither the scant biographical material nor the genesis of the poems support such a directly biographical interpretation;[11] instead these poems epitomize the nonconfessional nature of Meyer's poetry. His unfulfilled dreams about love are depersonalized and condensed in the basic figures of the dead beloved who is characterized — if at all — as a shy, untamed stranger in this world. Henel explains that unrequited love made Meyer keenly aware of his lacking access to life and that, consequently, he felt the need to picture this failure in the form of adverse fate, of death depriving him of his beloved before their love could mature.[12]

Death is important in another sense as well. By arresting the flow of life, by eliminating any further changes, it enables Meyer to contemplate his painful feelings from a distance growing with time. This contemplation turns into objectification, into art which — like death — isolates an experience from the transience of life and gives it lasting form. This view of art is crucial for Meyer and is illustrated in the poem "Michelangelo und seine Statuen" ("Michelangelo and His Statues") in which the sculptor addresses some of his works:

> Du öffnest, Sklave, deinen Mund,
> Doch stöhnst du nicht. Die Lippe schweigt.
> Nicht drückt, Gedankenvoller, dich
> Die Bürde der behelmten Stirn.
> Du packst mit nervger Hand den Bart,
> Doch springst du, Moses, nicht empor.
> Maria mit dem toten Sohn,
> Du weinst, doch rinnt die Träne nicht.
> Ihr stellt des Leids Gebärde dar,
> Ihr meine Kinder, ohne Leid!
> So sieht der freigewordne Geist
> Des Lebens überwundne Qual.
> Was martert die lebendge Brust,
> Beseligt und ergötzt im Stein.
> Den Augenblick verewigt ihr,
> Und sterbt ihr, sterbt ihr ohne Tod.
> Im Schilfe wartet Charon mein,
> Der pfeifend sich die Zeit vertreibt.
>
> You, slave, open your mouth,
> Yet you do not moan. Your lips are silent.
> You, full of thought, you are not weighted

By the burden of a helmeted brow.
With sinewy hand, you grasp your beard,
Yet you, Moses, do not jump up.
Mary with your dead son,
You cry, yet your tears do now flow.
You manifest the gesture of sorrow,
You, my children, without sorrow.
This is how the liberated spirit
Sees life's sorrow overcome.
What tortures the living breast
Elevates and delights in marble.
You render the moment eternal,
And if you die, you die without death.
In the sedge Charon waits for me
Who whistling whiles away the time.

The expression of emotions, however painful or violent they may be, acquires an artistic beauty that comes from detachment. In the act of creating the gesture of pain its acutest sting is already overcome. Released from the actual throes of suffering the artist is able to embody its vivid memory in a permanent form of consoling, even delightful beauty. The reference to Charon, however, indicates that such artists are always close to death, even in their active life.

Viewing his experiences of frustrated love through death and distance, Meyer produced a group of unusual love poems. Closest to the forceful expressiveness he admired so much in Michelangelo is "Wetterleuchten" ("Heat Lightning"). Here the pale face of the dead girl appears amid spring blossoms, and sudden flashes of heat lightning cast on her a glow reminiscent of her blushing "way back/When the first word of love startled you." In its short intensity this image symbolizes both the force of love and its early evanescence. A painting by Charles Gleyre (1806–1874) inspired Meyer, in "Lethe," to picture the dead beloved in Charon's boat gliding away from life. When the poet immerses himself in the water that has a "strange chill," when he tries to break into the boat, Meyer actually creates an image of himself and of his need to draw his poetry from the depths of death. As Henel shows in his interpretation, the beloved is also a symbol of Meyer's art, as is the boat gliding away noiselessly and without oars. This fine symbolism is, however, abandoned at the end where, for the sake of a dramatic conclusion, the beloved vanishes, leaving the poet empty-handed. Meyer did not bring this poem to full maturity, and it is thus very instructive in that it indicates how difficult it must have been for him fully to develop his unusual symbols without slipping back — as is the case here — into conventional imagery. Such imperfect poems set the accomplishment of others into full relief.

Felicitous unity of symbols and form is reached in "Stapfen" ("Footsteps"). Skillfully, Meyer develops another modest image into a suggestive symbol: returning alone from a walk with his beloved on a rainy day, the poet contemplates her footsteps which, imprinted in the wet soil of the woods, slowly disappear. The concluding lines read: "Fast unter meinem Blick verwischten sich / Die Spuren deines letzten Gangs mit mir" ("Almost under my glance vanished / The traces of your last walk with me"). The adjective "last" provides the key to the poem's subtle symbolism. The girl's vanishing footsteps presage her early death, the untimely end of a shy love. This adjective illuminates the significance of the girl's attributes: she is a guest at his neighbor's house, she is wearing a traveler's cloak and talking about another, longer voyage. Simple external circumstances thus become transparent for the transience of life. Her inner nature is characterized by such corresponding traits as "wandering, wayfaring, / Delicate, pure, dark as woods, but oh how sweet!" Again, an adjective opens up deeper dimensions: coining the compound "walddunkel," the poet endows the girl with an element of deep, yet charming reserve. As shown in the poems about the forest, for example, "Abendrot im Walde" ("Sunset in the Forest"), "Jetzt rede du" ("Now You Shall Speak"), and "Sonntags" ("On a Sunday"), the woods are for Meyer a realm of comforting refuge from the noise and the pains of the world. Congenial with the forest, the girl's nature is recondite, alien in the everyday world, and therefore all the more appealing. The description of her inner nature conjures up her delicate body before the poet's eyes; but it is "a dream figure" passing by. At the moment of intense recollection her strangeness too becomes palpable as the silent passing of someone whose footsteps, her contact with and imprint on the earth, are fading away.

The form of the poem is as light and unobtrusive as the symbol of the footsteps. Both language and vocabulary are evocative but never poetizing, and the rhymeless iambic pentameter lines prove to be marvellously pliable and quite soft despite their stressed endings. In addition, enjambments and an intricate syntax blur the metrical form, and this blurring perfectly corresponds to the main symbol, to the impressionistic light touch characterizing the entire poem.

Here as well as in "Der Blutstropfen" ("A Drop of Blood") Meyer infuses the iambic pentameter, the blank verse of the classical German drama, with a new lyric quality. In the most sensitive review published in Meyer's lifetime, Carl Spitteler wrote in 1891 about the poet's use of this verse: "The art to create a sublime mood — without any melody, solely with the images in words — in an unassuming meter ... has here reached absolute perfection.... And this art is new. Classical poets do not show us anything similar. Poems such as 'Stapfen' ... are in content and form of exemplary perfection and open new realms to lyric poetry for all times" (*W*, II, 39).

The beginning and end of "Stapfen" mark the poem's content as a remembrance. In "Der Blutstropfen," the temporal distance involved in remembering becomes visible in the symbol of the blood drop which, over the years, has faded but not disappeared. Tribute to the dead is the theme of "Weihgeschenk" ("Votive Offering") — a poem of a melodious charm rare in Meyer's entire lyric oeuvre — and of "Einer Toten" ("To a Dead Woman") where the poet's remembering is contrasted with the world's forgetfulness. For Meyer, remembrance is the main source of inspiration, both in the small scale of personal memories and on the larger scale of history. In "Chor der Toten" ("Chorus of the Dead") he expresses the significance of remembering:

> Wir Toten, wir Toten sind grössere Heere
> Als ihr auf der Erde, als ihr auf dem Meere!
> Wir pflügten das Feld mit geduldigen Taten,
> Ihr schwinget die Sicheln und schneidet die Saaten,
> Und was wir vollendet und was wir begonnen,
> Das füllt noch dort oben die rauschenden Bronnen,
> Und all unser Lieben und Hassen und Hadern,
> Das klopft noch dort oben in sterblichen Adern,
> Und was wir an gültigen Sätzen gefunden,
> Dran bleibt aller irdische Wandel gebunden,
> Und unsere Töne, Gebilde, Gedichte
> Erkämpfen den Lorbeer im strahlenden Lichte,
> Wir suchen noch immer die menschlichen Ziele —
> Drum ehret und opfert! Denn unser sind viele!

> We, the dead, the dead form greater armies
> Than you on the earth, than you on the sea!
> We plowed the fields with patient deeds,
> You wield the sickles and cut the seed,

> And what we completed and what we began
> Is still filling the rushing fountains above,
> And all our loving and hating and quarreling
> Still beats up above in mortal veins,
> And all earthly change remains bound
> To whatever valid maxims we have found,
> And our music, sculpture and poems
> Vie for the laurel in the glowing light,
> We still seek human goals,
> Therefore, honor and sacrifice! For we are many!

In the unusual form of four-stress dactylic lines rhyming in couplets Meyer forges a powerful rhythm and a solemn tone, resounding, as it were, with a multitude of voices. References to the dead "down here" and to the living "up there" regularly alternate, each reference filling one line, but every contrasted pair is tied into a single syntactical unit. Thus, the structure reinforces the idea that the dead with their deeds, thoughts, and emotions are inseparably bound up with whatever the living do, that the past inevitably conditions the present. "Chor der Toten" marks the point where Meyer's personal experience of death as an essential element in his life fuses with his interest in history. In other words, his way of seeing persons and feelings through a distance interposed by death, his emphasis on remembrance are the lyric equivalent of his proclivity for historical topics in his ballads and larger narrative works.

IV *Dionysian Life*

Yet there are other facets to Meyer's poetic world. The realm of the high mountains, evoked in many poems, is not only removed from the world as are the woods, it is also free of pain, of limitations; it is unimpeded by remembrance. The mountain landscape in the beautiful poems "Himmelsnähe" ("Close to the Sky") and "Noch einmal" ("Once Again") is striking in its combination of snow and ice, flowers, and rushing waters, all uniting to form an image of eternally living, timeless nature. In "Himmelsnähe," air and wind, the silence itself are felt as the spirit of life itself — breath, prayer, and divine presence at once. "Noch einmal" adds a quietly gliding eagle as a symbol of inner freedom experienced in such surroundings, of deliverance from earthly heaviness. Clearly, the mountain landscape is the symbolic place for the poem "Das Seelchen" mentioned earlier. Here the soul is free enough to be contemplated. It has acquired the lightness of a butterfly and a transparency which is not destroyed but enhanced by the red mottling symbolizing past earthly pain. In the sense of the Michelangelo poem this is another example of the poet's freedom to transform past suffering into a symbol of quietly radiant beauty.

Between the realm of dark waters and that of bright mountains there is the realm of the harvest characterized by vivid, even glaring colors, intense emotions, and dramatic contrasts. In compact form, "Schnitterlied" ("Harvest Song") illustrates the nature of this world. The scene with its vigorous work and the fervid emotions of the harvest celebration represents abounding life. But at this highpoint of life death, too, is near:

> Von Garbe zu Garbe
> Ist Raum für den Tod —
> Wie schwellen die Lippen des Lebens so rot!

> From sheaf to sheaf
> There is room for death —
> How the lips of life swell red!

The juxtaposition of life and death is also suggested by the thunder and lightning in the background. In "Erntegewitter" ("Harvest Storm") all these elements appear in an even more dramatic form. The blazing light of the lightning flashes and the girl's gesture of ebullient life — emptying a full glass in one gulp — are but momentary pictures immediately absorbed in darkness. The abrupt changes from light to darkness are designed to intensify exuberant life unmindful of anything else. The poem is a prime example of Meyer's monumental style which carries gestures, emotions, and contrasts to the extreme. The result here is highly theatrical, wrought with art — there are three flashes of lightning, two scenes with girls, the second one being an intensification of the first — but with such obvious intent that the exuberance is not really convincing.

An interesting companion piece is the poem "Auf Goldgrund" ("On Golden Ground"). Aiming at an image of quiet richness, Meyer here compares a harvest scene, bathed in the light of the setting sun, to medieval paintings in which "the saints, the praying / Shine on golden grounds." By thus borrowing heightened significance — "divine grandeur" (*heilige Würde*) — for life from art it becomes evident how important forms already condensed and stylized are from Meyer's art. In the light of art he more readily recognizes life's higher meanings. It is no accident that the external world started to fascinate him in Rome, where he was surrounded by great art and where the emotional expressiveness of a Southern people endowed even ordinary life with a sense of form. Paintings and sculptures often inspired poems, for example, "Die Narde" ("The Nard"), "Die Kartäuser" ("The Cartusians"), "Die gegeisselte Psyche" ("Psyche Flagellated"), "Der tote Achill" ("Dead Achilles"), and "Die Jungfrau" ("The Virgin"), in which Meyer presents life in a sort of double stylization. But only in the latter three cases does he succeed in giving the poems the formal ease and significance of their models. His tendency to view life in stylized forms produced the best harvest poem in "Vor der Ernte" ("Before the Harvest"). Although each of its stanzas is very obviously divided into two equal halves the image of the moon crescent creates an exquisite unity. The crescent of the moon suggests pure beauty, as forms and sounds fuse into a melodious celestial harmony. Below a warm Southern wind — the Föhn — tumultuously agitates the ripe fields symbolizing full, overwhelming life; while the beginning of the harvest indicates activity and tangible richness of the earth. The form of the crescent, repeated everywhere, unites the two contrasting halves. Emil Staiger points out that sky and earth are dissolved in nothing but curved lines and that, thus, the poem captures the moment "when life cools down to art, when nature is transfixed into ornament."[13] This very formal element in the way Meyer views life separates him in yet another respect from the immediacy of *Erlebnisdichtung* and connects him instead with the poets of the turn of the century — Stefan George, Rainer Maria Rilke, and Hugo von Hofmannsthal.

The juxtaposition of life and death in the harvest motif appears in a number of variations. In "Nach einem Niederländer" ("After a Dutch Painting") the bedizened bride about to be painted is contrasted with the master's just finished painting of his own young daughter on her deathbed. Again, the discrepancy is heightened by art: on the completed painting the pale beauty of death is accentuated by a flowerbud of deepest color symbolizing a life never to bloom, while the painter's visitors bursting with excitement already project the next work capturing exuberant youth. And the concise image of "Auf dem Canal Grande" ("On the Canal Grande") shows how the short span of loud vitality in the glowing sunlight soon fades into the long shadows of extinguished life.

The main variation, however, which becomes a major motif in itself, is the ambivalent figure of Dionysos or Bacchus. According to Greek mythology, he is the god of spring, of beauty, of orgiastic life, and the conductor of souls to the underworld, the son of Persephone. Other double-faced figures belong to the Dionysian realm: the bacchante described in "Vor einer Büste" ("Looking at a Bust") as having a touch of cruelty in her lovely face; Medusa, beautiful but deadly to her beholder ("Die sterbende Meduse" — "Medusa Dying"); and a winged Eros statue revealed as death extinguishing his torch ("Der Marmorknabe" — "The Marble Youth"). What in these lyric poems appears as a juxtaposition of extremes is transformed, in the ballads, into dramatic action and sudden change from intense life to death. "Pentheus" tells the story of Agave who, abandoning herself to the Dionysian orgy, kills her father Pentheus because he doubts the divinity of Dionysos. Using the name Lyaeus ("loosener") for the god Meyer points to his essential power to release men from all ties, both good and bad, making them express unreservedly their instantaneous desires and feelings. Therefore, he is also a god of art, of full, unrestrained expression which may, however, turn into chaos and destruction. Under the spell of Dionysos men scorn every limit: in "Der trunkene Gott" ("The Drunken God") Alexander the Great feels himself an almost divine master of the universe; yet a reminder of his human limitations — shown in his slight physical deformity — sends him into a deadly rage that transforms the rousing celebration into the silence of death. Yet Bacchic scenes and figures are not restricted to ballads with themes from antiquity, they occur in ballads with medieval and Renaissance themes as well (for example, "König Etzels Schwert" — "King Etzel's Sword," "Jung Tirel" — "Young Tirel," "Die Seitenwunde" — "Wound in the Side," "Cäsar Borgias Ohnmacht" — "Cesar Borgia Powerless"). Clearly, Meyer sees bacchic life as a timeless phenomenon fascinating and frightening at once; and while he might have admired the vitality and daring that nature denied him, he could not help but end all these scenes with death, thus implicitly manifesting his distrust of this life, however brilliant it may be.[14]

In the ballads, Meyer's representation of this bacchic life as well as of historical drama in a more general sense does not always avoid a cramped, mannered style, as the language and the rhymes are forced or too obviously dramatic. Yet in such pieces as "Der Ritt in den Tod" ("Death Ride"), "Das Geisterross" ("The Phantom Horse''), "Bettlerballade" ("Beggars' Ballad"), "Die Füsse im Feuer" ("Feet in the Fire") and "Die Rose von Newport" ("The Rose of Newport") the poet manifests his craftsmanship. In "Der Ritt in den Tod" a bacchic moment is captured most concisely and effectively. Though duels are prohibited by pain of death, a young Roman kills an enemy in a duel; his glorious triumph will be followed by his execution. Choosing the form of a monologue in couplets, Meyer expresses the young man's triumph in a powerful way. The dactylic meter with its four stresses starting with one or even two unstressed syllables creates a vigorous, almost galloping movement throughout the poem. Terse imperatives and exclamations, often filling only half a line, convey the speaker's boundless pride that prompted him to defy the law. And his feeling of victory coupled with the certainty of imminent death culminates in the grand gesture of raising his head in triumph before submitting to death, the ultimate limitation.

Most popular among the ballads, "Die Füsse im Feuer" is an excellent example of Meyer's dramatic art. Avoiding mannerism he here uses the disjunctive style with moderation and to maximum effect. Its irregular rhythm is well suited for the depiction of the storm at the beginning, but more importantly it corresponds to the way in which the King's courier is confronted with shreds of memory that, confirmed by the children's stare, combine to growing terror climaxing in the nightmare. At this point, however, in an ingenious turn, Meyer shifts the dramatic emphasis from the images of crude violence to the subtly indicated agony of the host's internal struggle. The surprise is dramatically complete because the host can enter the guest room through a jib door. The drama ends on a contemplative note contrasting the courier's easy reliance on earthly power and the Huguenot's hard-won acquiescence in divine will. Forgoing rhyme and regular stanzas and even blurring the fixed length of the lines (six iambics) with a varying syntax, Meyer provides the poem with a formal unity by repeating certain words and the image of the feet in the fire. Upon closer examination, the use of the fire marks the dramatic crescendo: first, it signals warmth and hospitality to the courier; then it awakens his memories; finally it spreads in the dream to a fiery sea devouring him, a metaphor for his terror, maybe even his bad conscience; and at the very end, the Huguenot's words "You have devilishly murdered my wife!" associate him with a hellish fire of hatred.

A masterful use of varying images and repetitions is displayed in

"Die Rose von Newport." King Charles I of England is presented in two mirror scenes that repeat a basic situation — his arrival in Newport, where a girl offers him the city's emblem, a rose. First, he comes as the young prince and future king amid flowers and cheers. The girl offering the rose is his, and the whole world seems to lie at his feet. Many years later he arrives as the king, but as a fugitive in the midst of a snowstorm, unheralded and unheeded. The world, once so welcoming, has turned into a forbidding precipice, the rose is now withered, and the girl offering it is begging. She is an outcast like him, and her face mirrors his own face and misery. Referring to the refrain of the first stanza "Tomorrow the linden trees will tell the tale / Of the defoliated rose of Newport" the reader can see this girl as his own child, but she can also be interpreted as a purely symbolic image of his own withered life devoid of promise and bliss. While the sequence, and even the structure of the images, remain the same in both stanzas, the poet allows for enough deviation in length to preserve an element of natural life within a strict form. The impression of vividness is also rooted in the unrhymed dactylic lines which produce a light rhythm appropriate to the cheerful ride at the beginning as well as to the hasty, aimless flight at the end. Looking back to "Der Ritt in den Tod," the other equestrian poem, we realize what different effects a skillful poet can achieve with the same form.

Meyer's ballads overwhelm the reader with a wealth of historical material, they span history from classical antiquity to the Reformation and the seventeenth century, introducing kings and crusaders, monks, reformers, artists, and lovers. They talk about noble passions, about piety and greed, fulfilled and thwarted love, and about many a death; they present a world built on wide knowledge and reading. This seems to indicate that Meyer is here commanding the rich world which his time expected to be the natural domain of the creative writer. And as the poem "Fülle" ("Abundance") at the beginning of the poetry collection shows, he accepted this view and wanted to conform to it. Yet his praise of the world's copious riches is not altogether convincing: the negative expressions — "enough is not enough," "enough will never ever be enough" — suggest that the poet's prime basis is not so much the direct experience of abundance as the lack of it which, in turn, incites a strong desire to reach out for the riches of life. This desire is certainly genuine and produces some excellent ballads, but it is only part of his creative personality. "Fülle" must be seen together with the following poem

"Das heilige Feuer" ("The Sacred Fire") that compares the poet to a priestess watching the sacred fire at the dead of night. Here, the poet is in austere surroundings; lonely and separated from the mainstream of life, he is intently bent on only one purpose: his art. And while neither poem alone can describe Meyer's entire work, "Das heilige Feuer" does describe the more fundamental part, for even in depicting the fullness of life he cannot draw on experience, on natural identification, but has to rely on his artistic sense, his intuition, observation, and reading.

V   *Architectural Form*

Form is a dominant aspect of Meyer's poetry. In the *Gedichte* of 1882 he uses a much larger variety of meters, rhyme patterns, and stanzas — including forms without rhymes and stanzas — than in his earlier collections. His persistence in recasting and polishing poems, in isolating and developing individual motifs is rooted in a deep concern to find the congenial form for ideas, images, and feelings, many of them alien to the literature of the time. And this working process demonstrates clearly to what an extent form can be improved by aesthetic reflection, and that a good poem is not only inspired but also "made." Or as Mallarmé once put it: "It isn't with ideas but with words that one makes a poem."[15] In contrast to the French symbolists Meyer practiced this conscious way of writing — he often called it "building" — without any theories, without knowing that he was engaged in something new. This very lack of theoretical foundation exacerbated his frequent doubts concerning the validity of his poems in terms of "life" and "truth" which for him were still tantamount to good poetry. In 1881, when he was giving the bulk of his poetry its final, often original and perfect form, the question of whether his poetry had true life still haunted him, as is shown in the poem "Möwenflug" ("Sea gulls in Flight"). The image of sea gulls circling a rock is so clearly reflected in the green water far below them that there is no difference between reality and its mere reflection, "that deceit and truth completely resembled each other." In analogy to this image the poet asks:

> Und du selber? Bist du echt beflügelt?
> Oder nur gemalt und abgespiegelt?
> Gaukelst du im Kreis mit Fabeldingen?
> Oder hast du Blut in deinen Schwingen?

And you yourself? Are you truly winged?
Or merely painted and mirrored?
Are you dallying in a circle with fabled creatures?
Or do you have blood in your wings?

While ending in a series of questions, the poem itself is the answer, for its unassuming beauty with its light touches of white, green, and grey has the quality of true art that naturally saturates an image with significance transcending intellectual constructs. The image used here is in itself a symbol of Meyer's art: the motifs of the deep water and the free-flying birds represent parts of his poetic world. His art has "blood," not in the sense of an immediate expression of personal feelings but in that of beauty clearly tinged with Meyer's individuality, in the sense of exquisite images that betray, in their elaborate composition, his recondite feelings down to their slightest vibrations. And one must not forget that form, the counterpart of the "blood," has a double function: while mitigating emotions and creating detachment it also provides the protective frame that allows expression of the deepest experiences.

The importance of formal structure also comes to the fore in the organization of the poetry collection as a whole. Meyer divided the poems he selected for the volume into nine cycles, which he entitled "Vorsaal" ("Antechamber"), "Stunde" ("Hour"), "In den Bergen" ("In the Mountains"), "Reise" ("Travel"), "Liebe" ("Love"), "Götter" ("Gods"), "Frech und fromm" ("Impudent and Pious"), "Genie" ("Genius"), and "Männer" ("Men"). As in *Romanzen und Bilder (Ballads and Images),* there is an obvious division between lyric poems (1–5) and ballads (6–9). Yet upon a closer look this genre distinction becomes blurred, because the lyric cycles contain some ballads, as the ballad cycles contain a number of lyric poems. Moreover, many narrative poems have little or no direct action — "Das verlorene Schwert" ("The Lost Sword"), "Die Söhne Haruns" ("Harun's Sons"), and "Das Auge des Blinden" ("The Eye of the Blind") to name just a few. An extreme is reached in "Der Ritt in den Tod" and "Die Rose von Newport" which represent but momentary glimpses of climactic situations. The development of these ballads confirms this: in the course of reworking the long, wordy poems of the 1860s, Meyer made them more compact and expressive and condensed their narrative content ever more into one dramatic situation charged with contrasts. Thus, even the narrative poems assume, over the years, more of the

static character typical for Meyer's lyric poems which so often present motionless images, memories transfixed by death, or scenes
perpetuated by an artist. This loss of dynamic, and the increasing
prevalence of static, forms indicate that elaborate art rather than
direct representation of life shapes this poetic world.

The cycles and their arrangement corroborate this, too. The
poems of the second through ninth cycles are arranged according
to subject matter in the broad sense suggested by the cycles' head-
ings and in the narrower sense of imagery common to several
poems within a cycle. Such juxtaposition has implications which
are typical for Meyer's poetry. The time when a poem was first
written or published is disregarded. The group of the three Venice
poems covers a time span of twenty-five years: "Venedigs erster
Tag" ("Venice's First Day") was published in 1864 in *Zwanzig
Balladen;* "Venedig" was written in 1881–1882; and "Auf dem
Canal Grande" was composed in 1889 and added to the fourth edition of the *Gedichte* in 1891. Further, the poems about the dead
beloved have no chronological sequence at all, as is shown by their
dates of composition: "Weihgeschenk," 1869; "Der Blutstropfen,"
1881; "Stapfen," 1865; "Wetterleuchten," 1880; "Lethe," 1860;
and "Einer Toten," 1873. Thus Meyer implicitly confirms that his
poetry is not to be read in a biographical light. Also, the juxtaposition of poems with common imagery or theme does not necessarily
guarantee a common or related significance. The group consisting
of "Die gegeisselte Psyche," "Der tote Achill," and "Der Musensaal" is put together because they were all inspired by sculptures
Meyer had seen in Rome, but they differ widely in their meaning,
and only "Der tote Achill" refers at all to Meyer's association of
death and art; while "Der Musensaal" proclaims an opposite attitude by picturing the muses freed from their calm sculptural attitudes and engaged in a passionate dialogue about the segments of
life assigned to each of them. In his *Conrad Ferdinand Meyer und
das Kunstwerk seiner Gedichtsammlung,*[16] Walther Brecht establishes meaningful relationships — such as parallels, contrasts,
supplements — for the sequence of all poems within a cycle.

Brecht made a very valuable contribution, since he was the first
to recognize the formal composition of the nine cycles, the first to
call attention to the fact that not only the poetry but also the
arrangement of poems is meant as a work of art. In his view, the
fifth cycle "Love" is the center, the inner sanctum, so to speak,
which is symmetrically surrounded by the cycles 1 to 4 concerned

with Meyer's personal life, the world of his own experiences, and the cycles 6 to 9 devoted to the wider realm of European history. The latter four cycles each span a certain period: "Gods," Greek and especially Roman antiquity; "Impudent and Pious," the Middle Ages with their mixture of pious endeavor and earthly passion; while "Genius" focuses on the Renaissance with its extraordinary artists and towering political figures, and "Men" centers on the Reformation period. This historical macrocosm has a counterpart in the first four cycles outlining the microcosm of the poet's own world. For Brecht, "Antechamber" offers an introduction indicating the main themes of the collection, that is, poetry, love, and death, "Hour" concentrates on the poet's immediate surroundings, the lake, the harvest in the fields, the woods — and the moods associated with them; "In the Mountains" and "Travel" show the expansion of Meyer's poetic horizons.

Yet for all of Brecht's insights this interpretation of the volume's structure is not entirely satisfying, because the fifth part does not quite fit into this symmetry of inner and outer world. Moreover, the poems of the first cycle not only lack a common subject matter, but they are also, on the whole, of a somewhat inferior artistic value. For this reason, Henel separates this cycle from the other eight which then evenly represent the personal world (2–5) and the historical world (6–9). Noting that the poems in "Antechamber" focus on unlived lives, frustrations, the "dream hoard" of poetry, Henel convincingly concludes that this part represents the mute stage of Meyer's life when he himself lived in a dream world and was unable to express his experiences.[17] The very difficulty of understanding the main concept for this first cycle shows again to what extent Meyer needed and used impersonal forms as a protective screen for his own world with its formless depths and its visions of extreme forces threatening with chaos. The volume's formal composition — described as "architectural" by Brecht, as a "temple" by Henel — functions very much like the form in a poem: it sets up a visible, clear form for a world that threatens to disintegrate. For Meyer, only form, visible, plastic images, and strict composition made individual expression possible.

The poem "Schwarzschattende Kastanie" ("Dark Shadowing Chestnut Tree") encompasses essential elements of Meyer's art in a beautiful picture:

Schwarzschattende Kastanie,

Mein windgeregtes Sommerzelt,
Du senkst zur Flut dein weit Geäst,
Dein Laub, es durstet und es trinkt,
Schwarzschattende Kastanie!
Im Porte badet junge Brut
Mit Hader oder Lustgeschrei,
Und Kinder schwimmen leuchtend weiss
Im Gitter deines Blätterwerks,
Schwarzschattende Kastanie!
Und dämmern See und Ufer ein
Und rauscht vorbei das Abendboot,
So zuckt aus roter Schiffslatern
Ein Blitz und wandert auf dem Schwung
Der Flut, gebrochnen Lettern gleich,
Bis unter deinem Laub erlischt
Die rätselhafte Flammenschrift,
Schwarzschattende Kastanie!

Dark shadowing chestnut-tree,
My wind-stirred summer tent,
You lower your far-flung branches to the water,
Your foliage thirsts and drinks,
Dark shadowing chestnut tree!
In the harbor cove the young are bathing
Quarreling or shouting in delight,
And children swim gleaming white
In the lattice works of your leaves,
Dark shadowing chestnut tree!
And when lake and shore merge in dusk
And the evening boat murmurs past,
There flashes from the ship's red lantern
A streak of lightning and wanders on the surge
Of water, like broken lettering,
Until beneath your foliage vanishes
The mysterious flame-writing,
Dark shadowing chestnut tree!

The refrain "Schwarzschattende Kastanie" builds an architectural frame around the poem with its unrhymed verses. This clear frame separates the poet's own place — close to the water — from the wider world outside. The children swimming in the sunlight, their cries of joy and quarrel suggest a life full of activity and passions. The evening scene with the boat and the red reflections on the dark water suggest that realm where life, light, and emotion flash up once more before vanishing into darkness. The poet tries to capture this bright life in his work but does not quite succeed; life vanishes too fast for him and leaves only the flaming signals on the dark waters; it has become a mysterious text with an elusive meaning.

The image of the broken inscription is significant in a larger context as well. For the later nineteenth century life grew ever more disintegrated and less comprehensible, and philosophers gave up trying to devise a unified system encompassing all of life's phenomena; characteristically, Nietzsche's work offers but parts of a philosophical system and is often structured in short paragraphs. And the individual feels increasingly lost among a growing mass of people and in the face of a fast developing technology. Disintegration of larger meaning into smaller, disconnected parts is reflected in Meyer's writing process that tends more and more to isolate individual motifs which, in addition, are often composed of originally separate elements. In this respect, he is remarkably close to the principle of modern poetry as outlined by Baudelaire: "Imagination decomposes the entire creation and, with the materials thus accumulated and disposed according to rules for which the origin cannot be found but in the deepest depths of the soul, imagination creates a new world, produces the sensation of the new."[18] Against this background of decomposing reality and recomposing it in a new way, the principle of deliberate formal structure is shown in its full importance. For structure, artistic form, endow life with significance that can no longer be derived from a direct, emotional identification with the world, an intuitive understanding. Meyer's poetry opens a door to this new art: he is conventional in his openly professed endeavors — to create true, full life — and in parts of his imagery — abundance, heroic gestures — but at the same time he is an innovator in using new creative processes and in extending the limits of lyric beauty far into the realm of death.

CHAPTER 7

A Place in the World

MEYER'S creative productivity reached its peak in the early 1880s: while busy preparing the first and second editions of the *Poems* he did not neglect his prose. In rapid succession he finished four novellas: *Plautus im Nonnenkloster* (*Plautus in the Nunnery,* 1881) *Gustav Adolfs Page* (*Gustav Adolf's Page,* 1882), *Das Leiden eines Knaben* (*The Sufferings of a Boy,* 1883), and *Die Hochzeit des Mönchs* (*The Monk's Wedding,* 1883).[1] They form a fairly coherent group because their protagonists are young men or women who are trying to find a place in the world that would correspond to their temperament. Theirs is a difficult quest against great odds, and only in one case, that of Gertrude in *Plautus im Nonnenkloster,* is there a happy ending. Meyer's preference for enclosing a story within a framework is evident in three of the four instances. Only *Gustav Adolfs Page* has a direct narrative and will be considered first, even though *Plautus im Nonnenkloster* precedes it in time.

I Gustav Adolfs Page

For Meyer, the Swedish King Gustav Adolf (1594–1632) was a hero long admired, a man of faith and principles — like Rohan — as well as of decisive and successful action. Since the late 1870s he had planned to make him the hero of a historical drama in the Schillerian vein (*W,* XI, 279). Instead he wrote, within a few months and upon a sudden inspiration (*W,* XI, 280), a short novella focusing mainly on Auguste (Gustel) Leubelfing, an eighteen-year-old girl who adores the king and becomes his page in lieu of her cowardly, anile cousin. Having spent her childhood with her parents in Gustav Adolf's army camps, Gustel is accustomed to

such life and is an excellent horsewoman. Nearsighted as Gustav
Adolf is — and historically was — he never suspects a girl in the
slender figure of his page. The king is presented as a truly impos-
ing, yet human figure whose heroic stature is but slightly tainted by
his dream of being, one day, the king of a Protestant Germany. For
two reasons Meyer was fascinated even more by Gustel's ambiguous figure. First, as Gustav Adolf's page she lives an exuberant
life: being near the adored king — in battles and skirmishes as well
as in his private quarters — she enjoys the highest life always on the
brink of death, and of potential humiliation if she should be discovered. In talking with the king about the motto "Courte et
bonne" ("Short and good"), she expresses her philosophy of life:
"I wish that all the rays of my life were assembled in *one* cone and
in *one* hour so that, instead of a dull dusk, there would be a short,
but dazzling light of happiness [which would] then extinguish like a
lightning flash" (*W,* IX, 181). And although Gustav Adolf considers this incompatible with his faith in God's providence, he, too,
wishes that God might take him away "at the height of his powers
. . . before he would become useless or impossible" (*W,* XI, 185).
For king and page, death suffered in the victorious battle at Lützen
near Leipzig signifies the sudden end of a full life.

Gustel's death seems the only solution to her deeply problematic
life which is the second reason for Meyer's fascination with the
idea. She has no suitable place in either of the two worlds she
knows. With her active and enthusiastic nature she does not fit into
the world of her uncle and cousin in Nuremberg, which is the epitome of a materialistic bourgeois existence entirely dominated by
the concerns for money and social status. Meyer's descriptions of
father and son Leubelfing at the beginning and at the end of the
novella constitute a scathing attack on the self-righteous bourgeoisie that measures everything — even Gustav Adolf's friendship
with the banker Leubelfing — in terms of money. There is no place
for Gustel's idealistic views regarding the king and the value of
valiant fighting for a cause. Yet as the king's page, in a challenging
and emotionally satisfying environment, she must be deceitful,
casting shadows on the king and her ideals. Karl Schmid interprets
the story as a precise reflection of Meyer's own attitude toward real
life and historical greatness, an attitude comprising a lover's
enthrallment as well as the clear awareness of not really belonging
to the desired world.[2] In this sense, the story expresses Meyer's own
feelings of not belonging to any established, accepted world,

whether one of bourgeois efficiency or of rich, dramatic life as presented in world history. Against this background, the story's plot is psychologically true and far from being as contrived as some critics have charged. If the work as a whole is not fully convincing, other features are to blame; for instance, the improbable and rather weak scene between Gustav Adolf and Wallenstein, and the implausible resemblance between Gustel and the duke of Lauenburg, who was believed, by some historians, to have murdered Gustav Adolf.

II Plautus im Nonnenkloster

Plautus im Nonnenkloster presents a brighter picture, although it is not without dark elements. While hunting for a Plautus codex hidden in a nunnery in eastern Switzerland, the Florentine humanist Poggio Bracciolini (1380–1459) also uncovers a faked miracle performed since time immemorial on the day a novice takes the veil. This discovery enables the novice Gertrude to reject monastic life without breaking her pledge to the virgin when she was a child; thus, she can return to the life she is really destined for, that of a wife and mother. As her despair in the night before her vows shows, life in the convent cell threatens this countrygirl with madness and thoughts of suicide. Reminiscent of Jutta in *Engelberg,* Gertrude's fate is tied to the important motif of the renegade monk or nun which runs through a number of Meyer's works: first of all in *Die Hochzeit des Mönchs,* marginally also in *Der Heilige* — Hans der Armbruster is a former monk— , in two fragments *Die sanfte Klosteraufhebung (The Gentle Secularization)* and *Der Schrei um Mitternacht (Cry at Midnight),* and in the poems "Die Novize" ("The Novice," in *Zwanzig Balladen*), "Eine Nonne werd ich nicht" ("A Nun I'll not become") which later was changed into "Die Korsin" ("The Corsican Girl"), and "Frau Agnes und ihre Nonnen" ("Lady Agnes and her Nuns"). Often this motif has been interpreted only negatively as expressing Meyer's aversion to ascetic tendencies in his childhood home, especially in his mother who, after her husband's death, wore nunlike dresses, but also in Cécile Borrel and his sister, whom he compared to a Catholic family's "monk" when she took up her work at the religious institution of Samuel Zeller.[3] Or the motif has been seen as an expression of his Protestant desire to see individuals freed from rigorous religious bonds. This, however, does not account for such positive monastic figures as Father Mamette in *Angela Borgia,* Pater

Pancrazi in *Jürg Jenatsch,* and the monks in the poem "Die Kartäuser" ("The Cartusians"). Henel rightly points out that this ambivalence in the motif is rooted in the fact that Meyer longed for both participation in active life and seclusion from the world.[4]

The Plautus novella, the fist of Meyer's works dealing with material from the Italian Renaissance, certainly celebrates life. Gertrude returns to simple country life with "sun and clouds, sickle and scythe, husband and child" (*W,* XI, 156). The framework story set in the Renaissance Florence of Cosimo de' Medici conjures up the vision of a rich, refined life enjoyed — as Meyer says in *Die Versuchung des Pescara* — "with the delicate fingertips of artistic sense" (*W,* XIII, 160). Moreover, by selecting the humanist writer Poggio as narrator of, and actor in, the story, Meyer bathes everything — the noble Florentine audience and the rustic world of a small Swiss convent — in the rich consciousness that delights in sophisticated allusions, in the naive power of Gertrude's emotions as well as in the coarser comic aspects of Brigittchen of Trogen, the boorish, practical-minded abbess of the convent. Throughout he uses effective contrasts which, in the structure of the plot, are coupled with correspondences: Poggio's excursion to the convent with the melancholy Anselino, Gertrude's lover, has its counterpart when Poggio, on his return to Florence, meets Gertrude and Anselino as a happy couple; the scene on the meadows where the "miracle" is announced, indeed advertised, is paired with the scene in church on the next morning when the deceit is exposed; Poggio meets Gertrude, calm and composed, on the eve of her vows, and again, on the following morning, in utter despair; and Poggio follows and prefaces these meetings with reflections on the miraculous and on conscience. Finally, at the apex of the story, Poggio twice meets the abbess: first, she denounces him as a book thief; then, scared by his knowledge of the fraud, she hands him the Plautus codex. Unobtrusive as this structure may be to the casual reader, it supports the impression of a unified whole, in which comic lights and serious reflections are beautifully blended.

III   Das Leiden eines Knaben

Unlike *Gustav Adolfs Page* and *Plautus im Nonnenkloster,* Meyer's next novella, *Das Leiden eines Knaben (The Sufferings of a Boy),* is again the result of a plan mentioned already in 1877 (*W,* XII, 315) and carried out in 1883. Meyer described this work as "a counterpart to Brigittchen" (*W,* XII, 315) — the sad story of young Julian Boufflers who cannot find his modest place in his world, the court of the aging King Louis XIV of France (1638–1715). Because of his father's views on suitable education and strict discipline Julian must stay and suffer in the Jesuit College instead of taking a modest army position that would correspond not only to his ardent wish to serve his king and country, but also to his limited intelligence and his only talent, his fencing skills. Meyer found the story in the memoirs of Saint-Simon, the merciless chronicler of the late years of the "Sun King's" reign. He was impressed by it because it allowed him, as he later admitted, to voice "more than anyone might think the moods of [my] anguished youth" (*W,* XII, 315). The story thus can be read in the light of Meyer's own life, but caution is necessary with such an assumption because he veiled the basic similarities by a number of dissimilarities.

As in the case of Meyer, it is taken for granted that Julian, the son of a respected marshal in the king's army, will follow in his father's footsteps, that he will complete his studies and gain a high army position. Unlike Meyer, Julian lacks the mental capabilities for this role, but like Meyer he finds himself in an environment where strictly disciplined work is believed to guarantee success in any endeavor. In the hard-working Marshal Boufflers we can see with David Jackson reflections of Meyer's father who, constantly overloaded with work, could give his son but little attention and might not have had — or taken — the time to discover his son's individual strengths and weaknesses.[5] In Julian's unsophisticated, but loving and understanding mother Jackson sees the mother whom Meyer needed but did not find in the highly talented Mrs. Meyer. Like the author, Julian is unable to defend himself, yet unlike Meyer he strains every nerve to meet his father's expectations, bearing humiliations of being left behind in school and of being maltreated by the Jesuits, who have come to hate his father. A corporal punishment, which deeply wounds Julian's sense of honor, precipitates his fatal illness.

Like Meyer, Julian does not and cannot express his pain except to the illiterate but genial animal painter Mouton who represents a so-called uncivilized but ultimately more human world. Julian finds refuge in art, in his secret drawing sessions with Mouton: "...even the illusions of a success, the participation in an ingenious activity, in an effortless and felicitous creation ... let the boy experience a great happiness after so many losses in self-confidence" (*W,* XII, 124). In his art Mouton intuitively grasps and masterfully reveals the depths of Julian's hidden sufferings. He pictures the boy fleeing, like Pentheus, "with an expression of deadly fright" from persecutors shown as "personified ideas, torments, torturing thoughts." He also shows him headed for a pathless rocky barrier "that, before one's eyes, seemed to grow like a dark fate" (*W,* XII, 135). Both the visionary image and the broken, haunted syntax used in this description betray a desperate inner state from which Julian's fatal illness and Meyer's breakdown of 1852 seem to be the only means of escape.

Yet by lodging his own experiences in a story removed in time and place and borrowed from another writer, Meyer also reveals his intention of transcending the personal realm and of conveying the basic experience of an individual pitted unfairly against social expectations that he cannot possibly meet. The story's setting at the court of the absolute monarch Louis XIV emphasizes the rigidity of the social hierarchy and the formal refinement of courtly life where Julian, in his simplicity, is both ridiculous and lost. In the Jesuits Meyer effectively portrays a reckless, destructive power system which has no consideration for anything or anybody that does not further its own political goals. Critics attribute this image to Meyer's Protestantism, yet this negative image stems less from a strong confessional stand — which Meyer lacked — than from his deeply individualistic distrust of any absolute attitude or system. In this story, a feeling for the individual, a true human concern are found in outsiders only — in the physician Fagon who, being of low birth, is nobody's competitor and enjoys a certain fool's license, and in Mouton who takes no note of society and the king. In Mouton's paintings of animals and in Fagon's occasionally uncourtly language, Meyer intrinsically criticizes form for form's sake that leaves no room for human consideration. How destructive mere form can be is shown in the figure of Julian's shy beloved; while she is frightened by Julian's appearance after his punishment (of which she knows nothing), her rhetorical preciosity, which she deems necessary for formal occasions such as the dinner in Versailles, provides the last blow for his crushed ego when she declares that "no subject of the proudest of kings will tolerate corporal punishment: a man thus stigmatized will not live any longer" (*W,* XII, 155).

As in *Plautus im Nonnenkloster,* Meyer chooses the form of a framework story, but makes a more special use of it by linking frame and actual tale so closely that the two are inseparable. Julian's story concerns not only the narrator Fagon, who was, like Poggio, an actor in the drama, but also his listeners: while the boy's sufferings deeply touch Madame de Maintenon, who was a friend of Julian's late mother, Fagon uses them to warn, indeed to criticize the king for his choice of Père Tellier, Julian's principal tormentor, as his new confessor. A drama unfolds between the king, who considers the tale as a pastime, and Fagon, who uses it for confronting the sovereign with a shocking reality. As W. D. Williams points out, the unveiling of past injustice is inextricably linked with Fagon's daring attempt to change the present.[6] The opposition between Fagon and the king is dramatically accentuated in the only interruption of the tale when the King flatly denies the reality presented by Fagon — that is, the coercion of Protestants to convert — because this reality is at variance with his concepts and orders: "no violence is used . . . because I prohibited it once and for all and because my orders are followed" (*W*, XII, 120). In a passionate, irreverent outburst, Meyer pits Fagon's experience of reality against the king's idealistic concepts, moral indignation against a principle of aesthetic moderation, when the king declares "Unhappy things want a veil" (*W*, XII, 121). Here Meyer criticizes form and excessive aestheticism which are likely, or even designed, to obscure unpleasant issues. By setting this climax very early in the work, he suffuses the remaining two-thirds of the story with a fundamental tension and a sense of urgency that otherwise would be missing.

Fagon fails to awaken the conscience of the king whose laconic reaction "poor child" classifies the story as an already closed, isolated incident; and this prompts Fagon, who has exhausted his passionate appeal, to a final comment ringing with bitter irony. Yet Fagon does not fail with the reader, who shares his concern and understands his shame about not having acted earlier and more decisively to protect Julian. Although at times the boy's remarks betray more intelligence than he is said to have, Meyer succeeds in transforming a story that could easily have smacked of the sentimental into a significant psychological drama which is as accomplished as it is moving.

IV Die Hochzeit des Mönchs

The year 1883 was the most productive in Meyer's career: within a few months after the completion of *Das Leiden eines Knaben* in July he brought to maturity another novella, *Die Hochzeit des Mönchs (The Monk's Wedding),* which he sent to the *Deutsche Rundschau* in October. Such a swift completion is all the more remarkable since the genesis of this new novella was complex and resulted in the most elaborate framework to be found in his oeuvre, indeed in the German novella as a whole. As mentioned above, the idea of the defrocked monk is connected to personal experience, yet Meyer experimented successively with such different settings as Corsica, the papal castle of St. Angelo, twelfth-century Nuremberg, and thirteenth-century Florence before finally setting it in Padua during the reign of the tyrant Ezzelino da Romano (1194–1259). From Macchiavelli's *Florentine Stories* he knew the tale of a young man who breaks his engagement upon the instigation of a jealous mother, quickly marries her daughter, and is then killed by the family of his former fiancée. As early as 1865–1866, he used the material for the poem "Der Mars von Florenz" ("Mars in Florence"), and its revision around 1880 might have revived his interest in the story. By combining it with the motif of a monk who is put under pressure to leave the monastery in order to marry his brother's widow, he weaved fate and passion into a work of dark and enigmatic colors.

Like *Der Heilige,* this novella has a deeply — and intentionally — puzzling character which is, even more than in the earlier work, sustained by a complicated framework. In direct contrast to Becket, Astorre Vicedomini abandons the realm of the church for the world, and like Gustel Leubelfing and Julian Boufflers he cannot find a place where he could truly, fully live. Yet while Gustel deals actively with her situation, and while Julian suffers it passively, Astorre's case is more complex, intertwining emotional pressure in his dying father's ploy to make him renounce his vows, the strange workings of chance or fate, and Astorre's own actions inspired by his passionate feelings. Meyer offers explanations on the levels of immanent justice, impersonal fate, and psychological motivation, and he so enmeshed the different elements that judging Astorre's actions and also defining Meyer's own stand is a difficult but fascinating task.

An essential component of the work's opacity is its form. Following the old Italian novella tradition, Meyer introduces a group of people, assembled around the ruler of Verona, Cangrande della Scala (1291–1329), his wife, and his mistress, who are engaged in telling stories as a pastime for a long winter evening. Dante (1265–1321), living in exile at Cangrande's court, joins them; he contributes a story which he is inventing on the spot from an epitaph — "Here lies the monk Astorre with his wife Antiope. Ezzelino buried them." Dante boldly borrows the names and external characteristics of his listeners for his tale: the audience provides the models for all the main characters, with the exception of Astorre — from Ezzelino (Cangrande) to Astorre's friends, the courtier Ascanio and the soldier Germano, to Gocciola, the fool. Thus, the listeners feel closely involved, so much so that Cangrande's wife and his mistress impulsively take sides with their respective figures Diana Pizzaguerra and Antiope Canossa. In doing so, they reveal themselves and elucidate the scene at hand which contrasts the two women: Diana, noble and sedate, but accused of being cold and insensitive, and the younger Antiope, delicate and tender, but reproached for being cunning (*W,* XII, 64).

At the same time, such closeness between audience and listeners is counteracted by repeated interruptions. Cangrande questions some of Dante's moral judgments (*W,* XII, 43–44) which are inconsistent and thus tarnish the poet's authority. At the very point where Astorre's passion leaps into flame after Antiope was struck by Diana, the listeners argue with Dante whether love is a matter of course or truly exceptional (*W,* XII, 63); and in the midst of Antiope's and Diana's final dramatic encounter Dante interjects speculations on what really happened (*W,* XII, 96). Several times Meyer breaks in on Dante's narration to indicate how masterfully the poet arranges details culled from his audience. These interruptions serve several purposes. First, they disrupt the empathy of both Dante's listeners and Meyer's readers, thereby creating distance and inviting critical judgment of the events, and of Dante himself. The reader is made aware of how difficult it is to judge events and to make moral judgments.[7] Second, the interruptions emphasize the fact that the tale is a work of art, consciously constructed, not immediately lived. And finally, they show how Dante adroitly sways his audience between closeness and distance, between identifying approval and critical reproval.

Dante himself takes a curious position. Though by inventing the story he would seem to be absolute master of his material and his characters' intents and motives, he refuses to pass judgment. Again and again he suggests different explanations — often phrased as questions—without giving so much as an indication as to which one would be closest to the truth. Dante's and Cangrande's exchange about a possible blasphemy of Emperor Frederick II (1194–1250) and the betrayal of his chancellor Petrus de Vinea develops this further: in both cases, Dante's judgment as expressed in his *Divine Comedy*, does not correspond to the one he would pass "according to his innermost feeling" (*W,* XII, 43–44). What matters here are neither Frederick's nor Vinea's actual deeds but the fact that Dante's public judgments in his work are relative, even dubious. In Meyer's view Dante, the writer has altogether ceased to be the respectable and respected arbiter of life by ceasing to be omniscient. He can invent stories that reflect true life but cannot explain all its mysteries or distill life's one and true meaning. Meyer's Dante has lost the belief in a basically meaningful order of the world and in the power of moral judgment; unable to provide answers, he and Meyer are confined to speculate about life from an external, limited point of view. Meyer establishes this attitude at the very beginning when Dante tells his audience that he will take the tale's characters "from your midst and give them your names: I shall leave your inner self untouched since I cannot read it" (*W,* XII, 12).

Under these conditions, it does not surprise that the story itself remains open to varied interpretations. The point that seems clearest is the end: Astorre's and Antiope's great love ends in chaos and destruction. Their love as well as Diana's revenge are Dionysian in nature, immediate self-expressions transgressing all barriers. Astorre and Antiope disregard Astorre's solemn engagement to Diana even in the face of the priest's refusal to marry them (*W,* XII, 75–76); and Diana, feeling wronged, disregards Ezzelino's order for peace, kills her rival, and precipitates Astorre's and Germano's death. Yet how is this end to be understood? Is it an example of immanent justice meting out punishment to the transgressing lovers, or is it the last link in a chain of events directed by an iron, enigmatic fate? How guilty is Astorre, who left the convent to save his father's soul from damnation? The standard interpretation takes Astorre to be guilty because he betrays monastic life — unquestioningly seen as his true nature and vocation — and consequently lapses into total inconstancy. Benno von Wiese puts forward the sophistic argument that Astorre violates his monastic obligation to be merciful by performing this mercifulness in the world — toward his father, toward Antiope — and not, more properly as a monk.[8] While finding the breaking of the monastic vows justifiable, W. D. Williams sees Astorre's guilt in his breaking his vow to Diana — which Williams, strangely enough, regards as "entered freely and deliberately" — "in a flush of sensual passion."[9] Fritz Martini claims that Astorre deserves punishment for disturbing the strict order which the world requries, but at the same time he assumes the existence of a dark fate creating an insoluble entanglement, which actually contradicts his assumption that some moral order exists.[10] Michael Shaw argues that Astorre is not really destined for, but merely accustomed to, his monkhood, and that in refusing to play a role as Diana's husband he is rebelling against a world which, neglecting the individual, simply substitutes one person for another, a "world not worth having."[11] What complicates the issue even further is the fact that the other characters are guilty, too: Astorre's father of avarice and deceit, Diana of an irascibility that prompts her to strike, and later kill, Antiope who, in turn, is guilty for consenting to an unlawful marriage; and Ezzelino is guilty of immediately sanctioning it. In addition, as Shaw suggests, society as a whole can be blamed for fostering questionable principles of action. The very possibility of such varying opinions indicates that Meyer aims less at defining the characters' exact guilt than at impressing upon the reader how difficult it is to pass an equitable judgment because our understanding — like Dante's — is limited, and because events and motivations are so extremely complex. David Jackson's psychological interpretation of the work illustrates this last point very well: focusing on certain features in Astorre's reactions that have been overlooked so far Jackson opens up yet another dimension.[12] The following brief discussion will touch on some of his main points.

Astorre's story revolves around two crucial scenes that are at once similar and different. In the first one, his dying father makes him renounce — reluctantly — his monastic vows and destines him to marry his brother's widow Diana. In the second scene, Germano's engagement to Antiope — simply intended as making amends to Antiope for Diana's offense — does not materialize. Astorre now willingly breaks his vow to Diana, again urged by a parent — Antiope's deranged mother Olimpia — and is now most anxious to have this new commitment sanctified. The two scenes bring about one of the sudden reversals with which the story abounds. Noting them, W. D. Williams observes that they create an atmosphere of uncertainty and fatality; but beyond that they also serve as dramatic reminders of the fact that well-known persons can have surprisingly different faces, that our view of reality and of life is incomplete. In Astorre's case, the reversals uncover and promote another part of his self that was hidden and repressed. The old Vicedomini's family egotism is notorious enough for Astorre, walking home from the accident scene, to overhear how the "rapidly calculating Paduans" speculate on whether the monk would leave the monastery to continue the family and preserve its wealth (*W,* XII, 18). Having heard this and knowing his father, Astorre can hardly be taken by surprise at his father's pressure on him; and his quick discovery of the fraud subsequently proves that he is neither an idealist nor a simpleton. Yet he yields, apparently acting on his feeling of compassion that seems most consonant with his monastic vocation. This, however, creates a paradox: the exercise of his monastic virtue terminates his monastic life, as Shaw rightly points out. The very existence of such a paradox suggests that Astorre might have another, subconscious motivation for which David Jackson offers further evidence. He calls attention to Astorre's shy, awkward behavior toward Diana at the scene of the accident and to his sudden aversion toward her when she reveals herself as "a rougher and more real figure than the delicate appearances of the legends. He had imagined women to be softer" (*W,* XII, 31). More startling is the observation that, when she is kneeling before the old Vicedomini, Diana's neck resembles that of Antiope lying on the block next to her father's — the very image that for three years had never left Astorre's mind (*W,* XII, 66). Therefore, it is plausible that behind the obvious reasons for Astorre's renouncement — pressure, religious beliefs, compassion — there is also an unacknowledged desire to leave the monastery.

Astorre's memories are revealing, too. A casual remark recalls them in such intensity that they blot out everything else. According to Jackson, they also suggest that, for Astorre, love is connected with and inspired by pain and torment. Thus Diana's blow, intended for the insulting Olimpia, but received by Antiope, must dramatically fan his hidden and still forbidden love. It is indicative that in his love monologue Astorre rapturously relives the moment of Antiope's maltreatment (*W,* XII, 66). Jackson also points to the passage where Dante approvingly links profoundest compassion with highest love by referring to Christ: "...the Divine, too, was beaten, and we kiss His weals and wounds" (*W,* XII, 71). Under the veil of Dante's approval Jackson detects Meyer's wish to question this bond between pain and love which is so typical for Christianity, so typical, too, for the attitudes Meyer encountered in the environment of his youth. Pursuing this line of reasoning, Jackson supposes that the fatal ending of Astorre's and Antiope's love may even have been subconsciously desired by Astorre. Indeed, by choosing a tragic end after having provided for a happy solution, Meyer seems to indicate that this love and these lovers could not survive in the world for both ethical and psychological reasons. Astorre and Antiope transgress the minimal order necessary to sustain society, and Astorre seems unable to break himself of what Asconio calls "the monkish way of either idolizing or despising [women]" (*W*, XII, 36). He seems unable to adjust to a love geared to simple enjoyment and unwarped by pain. Jackson's observations thus enrich our understanding of the work in two ways: they show that Astorre had a subconscious desire to leave the monastery and therefore was not quite the exemplary monk he was believed to be; and they show that his love is of a questionable, disturbing nature, which is, however, conditioned by the environment and by traditional attitudes.

Jackson's approach also sheds some light on the incidents on the bridge. Still inwardly vibrating from the intense memories of Antiope at her father's execution Astorre must buy a ring for Diana. His hesitation between a larger and a smaller ring reflects his divided loyalties. And when, looking for the small lost ring, he suddenly meets Antiope wearing this very ring, his emotions prevent him from even attempting to explain the real situation before he is dragged away by Germano. It is Astorre's psyche, his inner excitement, that play a major role here by determining his actions or nonactions, and because of this he attributes momentous significance to this meeting with Antiope. Thus, in some of the story's so-called "fateful" incidents fate plays a lesser part than the person's psyche. The story of Ezzelino's illegitimate son is a case in point: when discovering the reason for the tyrant's unusual pardon, his soul is poisoned, he rebels again, and is killed (*W*, XII, 83). This way of viewing fate as coming from inside and as being determined by one's own psyche, reflects Meyer's extensive reading of the German romantics in his youth, and especially Novalis' opinion that "the world eventually becomes the soul [*Gemüt*],"[13] that man's inner state is a principal force in shaping external events.

There remain, however, instances of striking coincidence such as the accident on the river, the fact that Antiope and her maid are at the very spot where the rolling ring can be seen and be picked up, and the presence of a priest in the Canossa chapel. Meyer makes no attempt to elucidate them; rather, he uses them to show a mysterious force in life that is beyond human comprehension and control. Another manifestation of this force is death, which plays such an important part in the story. No wonder that Ezzelino, aspiring to be an absolute ruler is so attracted to death scenes. Entering houses unannounced, imperturbably watching the deaths of his subjects, and boldly sanctioning — against existing laws and morals — Astorre's sacrilegious marriage, Ezzelino envelops himself with an aura of absolute power. But he, too, is beaten by the final events, and Dante uses him as a warning to Cangrande that power itself is powerless.

Die Hochzeit des Mönchs is Meyer's most idiosyncratic work. With the exception of Astorre the characters in themselves are quite simple, since they embody, in the words of Ernst Feise,[14] only their dominant passion. The old Vicedomoni exemplifies avarice, Germano absolute loyalty to his master and his orders, Ascanio cheerful enjoyment of life, Diana proud directness and realism, Antiope the sentient abandon of tender youth. Thus the characters resemble woodcuts or puppets in a traditional puppet play. Yet their simplicity is sharply contrasted and ingeniously combined with events that are complex and enigmatic, thus adding the intriguing interest which the characters themselves do not engender. And all this is encased in a most elaborate form, which allows Meyer to present a world with complex, open-ended meanings that defy a clear definition of guilt and innocence. In this presentation, the enigma of the events indicates the difficulty of passing judgment.

Whatever interpretive line the reader chooses to stress, the work remains a dark and disturbing one. It is therefore worthy of note that Meyer wrote this novella at the time of his greatest external happiness: since 1879 he had been unusually productive and had established himself as a major writer. He had a family, was well off, had regained a respectable position in his native Zurich, and he was free of illness. Yet the four works discussed in this chapter, and especially *Die Hochzeit des Mönchs,* reveal that, deep down, he did not feel at ease in this comfortable bourgeois idyll and knew he had no real place in it. The bourgeois framework, however, was a necessity for him: by being anchored in a firmly ordered external world he was able to explore the dark realm behind it where its own values become ambiguous, where even love may become a frightful aberration. Because of such disparity, the complex framework and the creation of ambiguous meanings were indispensable.

CHAPTER 8

The Hidden Wound

WITH *Die Hochzeit des Mönchs* Meyer reached a *non plus ultra,* the ultimate form of the framework story. He agreed with friends and critics that in proceeding in this vein he would risk mannerism (*W,* XII, 251–52); therefore, he returned to the simpler form of unframed stories in his last completed works, *Die Richterin* (*The Judge,* 1885), *Die Versuchung des Pescara* (*The Temptation of Pescara,* 1887),[1] and *Angela Borgia* (1891). In these novellas, however, he continued to portray a perplexing world characterized by discrepancies between the external appearance and the true nature of people and situations. It is a measure of Meyer's mounting pessimism that he chose as protagonists characters like Stemma, the judge, and Pescara: well established in the world, they are in a position of command that they use responsibly; yet the stories reveal that they each have a hidden wound that limits their ability to solve problems. Only in *Angela Borgia,* which is a work of quite a different character, the hidden wound of Angela's moral rigor and the open one of Giulio's wasted youth are healed so as to form the basis for a new, balanced life.

I Die Richterin

While plans for *Die Richterin* go back to 1875–1876, the project cannot be traced before 1881 (*W,* XII, 342). Developed at the same time as *Die Hochzeit des Mönchs,* this story is also envisioned as taking place in the Sicilian environment of Emperor Frederick II; fragments of this plan, written in late 1883, are preserved (*W,* XII, 353–65). Yet finally Meyer chose to set the work in Graubünden at the time Charlemagne was emperor (800–814). In this region and period he found, as he wrote to L. von François, "the wide space and wild customs" he felt were needed as a foil for the story's

137

"somewhat large figures" (*W,* XII, 345) who are involved in administering justice, but also in murder, deceit, and possibly incest. The three main characters are indeed of a heroic kind. Having inherited the judicature in early years, Stemma has resolutely and ingeniously instituted order and justice in her domain, which had been racked by family feuds and is still disturbed by roaming hordes of Lombards. But she began this task after having secretly poisoned her much older husband, whom she doubly abhorred because she was already pregnant by Peregrin, a young traveling scholar murdered by her father. Striving for justice, she herself hides from it and even denies the truth to her daughter Palma Novella, who happened to overhear her when she defiantly hurled the naked facts at her husband's grave. Stemma's stepson Wulfrin is one of Charlemagne's warriors; he is strong, courageous, and as violent in his passion for Palma Novella, whom he believes to be his "half-sister," as he is in his guilt about this seemingly sinful feeling. Palma, endowed with an undaunted, adventurous spirit, first innocently indulges in her love for the admired "brother," but when she realizes the depth of her feeling and learns the truth of her birth, she refuses to live knowing yet dissembling the dark secret.

Counterparts to these strong-willed characters are the Bishop Felix of Chur who, in his Christian meekness, is unable to assert his authority, and his "nephew," that is, natural son, Graciosus, who is a self-righteous coward; for although he wooed Palma he does not want to marry the child of a murderess. Stemma is given a parallel figure in the servant Faustine, who also killed her husband because she was already pregnant by a dead man; but once her daughter is married she confesses her crime to Stemma and demands her rightful punishment. Above them all Charlemagne rules as supreme judge, a personification of just and forceful order. The contrast between Bishop Felix, on the one hand, and Stemma and Charlemagne on the other, implies a veiled political statement. For Meyer, Stemma's Graubünden as well as his own restless world seemed to require a strict rule of law and order rather than the bishop's idealistic belief in the goodness of human nature, a belief incidentally, which was advocated by Tolstoi, whose book *My Religion* Meyer read with great interest when working on *Die Richterin* in 1884–1885.[2] But by revealing Stemma's shortcomings, Meyer avoids an unqualified glorification of authoritarian rule. In other words, though sympathetic to the government of Bismarck's

Germany he did not admire it unconditionally.

Set farthest back in the past among all of Meyer's works, *Die Richterin* is nevertheless very modern in content. While, from a realistic point of view, the characters may appear oversimplified and the plot contrived,[3] these features are plausible when viewed as symbolizing psychological phenomena, as translating the difficult emergence of repressed and subconscious feelings — Stemma's guilt, Palma's and Wulfrin's love — into a story. As a matter of fact, Sigmund Freud was so fascinated with this work that in 1898 he chose it for his first analysis of a literary text.[4] Though quite technical, Freud's analysis stresses some points that are also useful for a general interpretation. Without knowing Meyer's biography,[5] Freud confirms Betsy's remarks — first published in Volume 12 of the historical-critical edition (*W*, 340–41) — that the work constitutes Meyer's defense against suspicions of an incestuous relationship with his sister, since it closely follows the common pattern of such "family romances" that are invented as a means of coping with problems in family relationships. In this case, the love for the sister is legitimized by revealing her illegitimate birth. While it seems impossible to determine whether Meyer and Betsy were ever physically intimate, as Freud supposes, it is indisputable that they were unusually close, sharing not only their daily life from 1857 to 1875 but — more importantly — the devotion to an artistic vocation and a literary work that for so long seemed to be a phantom. In the beautiful poem "Ohne Datum" ("Undated") Meyer says that Betsy's faithful companionship was "the peace in this rush and flow / Of time" and that she alone was truly familiar with every detail of his work. The task of grappling with this complicated and hidden relationship leads Meyer, almost naturally, to create simplified figures who clearly represent certain attitudes at the cost of carefully shaded and more realistic descriptions. Thus, Charlemagne is needed as the remote, almost cherublike guarantor of order in a world of confusion, Wulfrin must be crushed by passion as well as by guilt, and Palma must be most engaging in her naive love, unaware, for quite some time, of its real significance.

In addition, Freud's purely psychological remarks about Faustine and Wulfrin's horn draw our attention to the more varied literary use Meyer makes of these features. Often criticized as too obvious a parallel, Faustine's confession serves as an unequivocal foil to Stemma's ambiguous feelings both about her love and her guilt. In her love for Peregrin, desire mingles with defiance and contempt. In contrast to Faustine, she continues to justify her impunity: she must not shake her people's confidence in justice, and she wants Palma Novella, the new life that sprang from death (*W,* XII, 219–20), to remain pure, ignorant of her true origin. When she finally confesses, she is too proud to submit to the judgment of others and judges herself by committing suicide. Meyer actually presents a psychological view of justice: after years of dissimulation Stemma betrays herself in a moment when she is disturbed by the unexpected, eerie sound of Wulfrin's horn which, the day before, she had thrown away. And when Palma would rather die than consciously hide her mother's secret, Stemma loses her main purpose in life — to see Palma happy — and feels she may as well confess. Paul Heyse is quite right in saying that this course of action diminishes the effect of conscience as an independent ethical force (*W,* XII, 349); but to the modern reader Meyer's explanation proves to be remarkable for this very penetration of the highly mixed elements that make up the phenomenon of "conscience."

Meyer uses Wulfrin's horn and the goblet as the main symbols throughout the novella. The horn, which is said to call forth admission of wrongdoing (*W,* XII, 166), is a symbol of judgment. Stemma hears its sound with discomfort because it reminds her of her husband's return when she poisoned him. Throwing the horn away becomes for her a "symbol of acquittal" (*W,* XII, 199); but this act, just like Wulfrin's symbolic absolution of Stemma before all her people, actually symbolizes her conscious design to hide the truth. The horn is retrieved from the depths of the gorge, and its sound in the middle of the night prompts Stemma to put her secret into words, thus precipitating the real judgment. The goblet is a symbol of love and union, but it has been misused in the poisoning; and only in the future will it again fulfill its true function as the answer of faithful love to the horn announcing the husband's return (*W,* XII, 235). Separated since the death of Stemma's husband, horn and goblet point to the discrepancy between external situation — Stemma's "marriage," Wulfrin's and Palma's relation as siblings — and inner truth — Stemma's murder and the children's legitimate love. Together, horn and goblet will symbolize the lawful and loving union of Wulfrin and Palma.

Despite this subtle use of symbols, Meyer does not succeed in fully linking the story's main topics, justice and incest, the latter of which has no basis in fact. And the first chapter, taking place in Rome, is a rather farfetched introduction which is not integrated into the tight structure of the remaining four chapters. The work contains powerful and evocative scenes — especially the guileless and yet erotic love scene on the mountain pasture in Chapter 3, and Wulfrin's despair when he walks through the gorge in the midst of a storm in Chapter 4; but it lacks the formal and intellectual unity Meyer achieved in his other novellas.

II Die Versuchung des Pescara

All through the 1880s Meyer pursued two large projects: a drama about the Emperor Frederick II and his chancellor Petrus de Vinea, and a novel *Der Dynast (The Dynast)* treating the long war of succession between Zurich and Schywz that troubled the Swiss Federation from 1436 to 1450. Yet these projects were never completed; repeatedly, they were superseded by other, often newer ideas. Thus, in 1886, the novel was set aside in favor of a novella about Fernando Avalos, the marquis of Pescara (1489–1525), a general in Spanish service who won a great victory over France in the battle at Pavia in 1525. Half Spanish and half Italian, he was asked to become the military leader of an Italian conspiracy against the Spanish Emperor Charles V and thus help to build an Italian state free from Spanish dominion. While the historical Pescara joined the conspiratory league *pro forma,* then executed the emperor's orders and suddenly died, Meyer's Pescara does not go that far: knowing — but hiding the fact — that his wound received at Pavia is fatal, he is basically beyond any temptation, even the possibility of winning the "dream crown of Italy" (*W,* XIII, 170). The work, entitled *Die Versuchung des Pescara (The Temptation of Pescara),* was completed in 1887.

The material appealed to Meyer for two reasons. First, it gave him the opportunity, as he wrote to Rodenberg on December 30, 1886, "to embody the types of the Renaissance" (*W,* XIII, 371), to describe the figures who made history in this fascinating period. There are the princes and diplomats with their Machiavellian politics: though representing the Prince of Peace and a spiritual empire, the pope is engaged in preparing a new war; the Florentin Guicciardino serves the pope, but sympathizes with Luther's reformation, and young and unstable, the duke of Milan, Francesco Sforza, demands and denies the conspiracy for the sole reason of preserving his own shaky position. Ambiguity and cunning culminate, however, in Sforza's chancellor Morone, who plays a major role by suggesting that Pescara be tempted, and by actually proposing betrayal of the emperor to Pescara. Unscrupulous, endowed with a protean nature, he is an ingenious politician. With masterly skill Meyer makes Morone a virtuoso of persuasion and dissembling, investing him with an astutely calculated eloquence which, in the temptation scene, rings with Morone's only deep, constant feeling, his love for Italy. In a pronounced way Morone represents both the dubious nature of Renaissance ruthlessness and the captivating quality of Italian eloquence, thus mirroring Meyer's divided feelings about the Renaissance. Only the poetess Vittoria Colonna, Pescara's wife, is a basically positive figure, constant in her love and dedicated to an art that combines beauty and ethical values. But like Gustav Adolf, she, too, is tainted by an egotistical desire, namely, to see Pescara liberate Italy and become king of Naples or even of Italy. Principled and untouched by politics, she embodies an especially dangerous temptation by sanctioning the proposed betrayal with her integrity and high sense of patriotism.

Pescara is surrounded by a group of different figures, mainly Spaniards. There is Leyva, a commoner general of unpolished directness; there is Pescara's young, noble nephew Del Guasto, a Don Juan type, who ruthlessly plays with and destroys women; while Moncada, sent by the Spanish court to spy on Pescara, represents the Loyola type, being highly refined yet frightening in his religious fanaticism that engenders cruelty. In the background looms the shadow of Emperor Charles V, ungenerous, melancholy, and inclined to somber piety. All these men stand for an empire of "slaves and henchmen" (*W,* XIII, 253) and embody the types of the emerging Counter-Reformation in which the Renaissance concept of the human being as an individual in his own right is consumed by a total subordination to an absolute political and religious power. Finally, there is the Frenchman Charles of Bourbon, once one of the most powerful men in France, but now infamous for having betrayed his king. Impeccable in his deportment and in fulfilling his duties in the Spanish army, he is the man of perfect form behind which he hides the emptiness of a deeply cynical view of himself, of mankind, and of the world.

The second reason for Meyer's fascination with the Pescara material lies in the fact that the plot itself, the very development of the events, is equivocal. The situation is one of suspense: an imperial ultimatum demands that the duke of Milan stay neutral and not join the Italian league if he is to avoid an occupation of his duchy by Pescara and his troops. Under this threat the Italian League must win Pescara as its leader. Using public opinion and Vittoria Colonna, Morone tempts Pescara, who is, at the same time, surrounded by growing distrust from the Spanish side. All but the sixth and last chapter deal with the waiting period before Pescara makes his decision, that is, before anything happens. Instead of external action, the story shows internal suspense, feverish maneuvers behind the scene, a political and psychological tug-of-war. In the midst of all this activity, Pescara is passive, motionless; a man of action and the man expected to move this entire world, he is now close to death and "beyond all earthly possibilities" (*W*, XIII, 242). Accordingly, the action has a dead center. Here Meyer is able to combine his liking for complex action and his inclination to withdraw from life: at the end of his life, Pescara is both a man of effective action and of disenchanted contemplation.

The would received at Pavia broke Pescara's strength, and his increasingly clear knowledge of imminent death shaped his unwavering attitude. To Vittoria he says in Chapter 4: "For a long time I knew the temptation, I saw it coming ... I did not waver, not for one instant, not with the slightest thought. For no choice has approached me, I did not belong to myself, I was beyond all earthly possibilities" (*W*, XIII, 242). In view of this confession, contemporary readers as well as later critics have questioned the appropriateness of the work's title. While it has been said that the word "temptation" is meant ironically or that Pescara's delay in answering Morone indicates a wavering,[6] the only convincing explanation applies the word not to Pescara but to Morone's and Vittoria's attempts to tempt him. Much of the singular fascination of this work stems from this unusual twist: that the temptation is directed toward a man who can no longer be tempted. In a letter of November 30, 1887, to L. von François, Meyer confirms this fact: "His fatal wound *preserves* [Pescara] *fataliter* from betrayal. Here everything is necessity" (*W*, XIII, 377). Yet this raises other questions: why does Pescara "feign life so well that Italy [offers him] her wedding ring" (*W*, XIII, 246)? How are the virtues of loyalty and justice, which Pescara mentions repeatedly, to be assessed if everything is destined? And what are we to make of "the ennobling of [Pescara's] character through the closeness of death" that Meyer adduces in a letter (November 5, 1887) to Haessel (*W*, XIII, 376)?

Pescara's alleged change from being "treacherous, cruel, and greedy" (*W*, XIII, 165) to being pious, obedient, just, and generous has often been overstated. Meyer neither provides insight into Pescara's earlier attitudes nor does he portray a change within the story. And as Michael Shaw's lucid analysis shows, Pescara is far less virtuous than it seems, so that this story "in appearance the most balanced, is actually the most hopeless and despairing."[7] Of course, Pescara demonstrates a certain political loyalty to the emperor, and in his treatment of the duke of Milan, in his refusal to execute Moncada's order that "terror reign in Milan" (*W,* XIII, 226) he is just. Yet taking a closer look at him Shaw persuasively shows that these virtues are only relative and thus somewhat questionable. This becomes evident when Meyer, in Chapter 3, offers the following explanations for Pescara's friendship with Bourbon: "Was it prudence, was it indifference toward ethical issues, was it freedom of every, even the best founded prejudice, or was it the highest justice of a perfect knowledge of human nature, whatever — Pescara had received the traitor with open arms..." (*W,* XIII, 199). All of these explanations have a common denominator in a moral relativism that judges people and situations not according to absolute standards but according to circumstances. Ambiguity also surrounds Pescara's loyalty: he is loyal to the emperor but "shudders at this Spanish empire: slaves and henchmen" (*W,* XIII, 253). In other words, his loyalty serves a regime that has become abhorrent to him. Moreover, in the case of Del Guasto he deems loyalty to the emperor to be the only way that would keep this cruel young man from becoming a criminal (*W,* XIII, 229–30).

If facing death changes anything in Pescara it sharpens his perception of political realities. He recognizes the faults of both his countries: Spain is strong but cruel and unjust, Italy degenerated and dying, but at least more human. Neither one holds a promising future for him: in Spain, his position is being undermined by "envy, creeping calumny, frail court favor," whereas in Italy he must expect "hate and poison for the man who rejected her" (*W,* XIII, 252). Because of this he says to Vittoria: "I am perishing of my victories and my glory. If I were without my wound I still could not live" (*W,* XIII, 252). Shaw concludes that by opting for loyalty to Spain, Pescara is ultimately loyal to his original decision to serve Spain rather than Italy: "he validates his entire past life."[8] For Pescara, the loyal discharge of his duties has lost most of its vital content and is rooted in disillusionment that leaves but one meritorious course of action: to avoid total chaos by adhering to the forms of loyalty even though its content is highly questionable. Pescara stops short of nihilism, but at the peak of his life death is his only way out; what seemed to be an abundant harvest of fame reveals its near emptiness.

Controlled form is an essential element of the novella. It finds expression in Pescara's masking his true condition with the image of life, in his upholding the forms of justice and loyalty while having lost his belief in them. Form is also most obvious in the work's symmetrical structure and its elaborate symbolism. Interpreters have always pointed out that the first five chapters equal the structure of a classical drama with the exposition in the first and the climaxing confrontation between Pescara and Morone in the third chapter after which action and tension are falling. The sixth chapter — deliberately entitled "last chapter" — constitutes an epilogue; it describes the drama's consequences and contains the only external action. But it has not been noticed so far that the six chapters, taken together, provide another symmetrical structure. Chapters 1 and 2 prepare the temptation, chapters 3 and 4 focus on the temptation as undertaken by Morone and Vittoria, and chapters 5 and 6 explain its failure. Imagery relating to life and death underlies and strengthens this tripartite structure. Images of life prevail in the first part: there are the frescoes in Sforza's palace presenting a bacchanalian feast and the feeding in the desert; there is the painting of Pescara and Vittoria that charms the contemplators with "the high and tender love which blended the soft features of the poetess and the hard ones of the general into warm life" and with their youth, "for the scarred and tanned Pescara appeared as a heroic youth" (*W,* XIII, 159–60). The second chapter is filled with the promise of a brilliant vision of Pescara as the leader and creator of a new Italy. This vision is, of course, also an essential part of the following two chapters, but it is counterbalanced by hints of death crystallizing first in Pescara's cryptic summary of his conversation with Morone as a "tragedy" entitled "death and fool" (*W,* XIII, 215) and culminating in the revealing of his true condition to Vittoria at the end of the fourth chapter. In the last two chapters death prevails: there are Pescara's symbolic confrontations with the Swiss lansquenet who wounded him at Pavia, whom he sees first *in effigie,* on a newly painted altarpiece at the Convent of the Holy Wounds, and then in reality; there is also Pescara's gesture describing his future with the ashes he holds in his hand. The last chapter unfolds the death component of the harvest motif: victory and power fall into ruin, the victor dies at noon, and Meyer likens the dead Pescara to "a young, slender harvester sleeping on his sheaf exhausted from the harvest" (*W,* XIII, 275).

The novella describes a circle starting and ending in Milan and with harvest imagery. Yet the course of the story leads the reader from the harvest as an image of life to the harvest as an image of death. Pescara simulates life while knowing that he is dying, while even yearning for death. This can be seen as expressing resignation in the transience of life. But Meyer goes even farther: Pescara preserves only the external forms of loyalty and justice while realizing that his loyalty supports a system that tramples justice under foot and that justice cannot survive in either Italy or Spain. Viewing Pescara's virtues as forms stripped of their essential content also helps us to understand Meyer's use of Christian imagery. The altarpiece in the Convent of the Holy Wounds suggests a symbolic relation between Christ and Pescara, since the Swiss lansquenet served as model for the soldier who opens Christ's side. When shortly afterward Pescara sees this same Swiss being attacked by Spanish soldiers, he not only enables him to pass through the Spanish lines but also gives him a full purse, thus practicing generous forgiveness. This has induced interpreters to see him as an imitator of Christ, thus giving his life a Christian meaning and elevating his loyalty and justice to exemplary virtues. Such an interpretation, however, does not quite tally with the fact that Pescara is described as an unbeliever who is known to avoid any Christian places (*W,* XIII, 248–49). The Christian symbols, too, are forms devoid of their religious significance. For Pescara is no Christ-like figure, as he despairs of a brighter future and sees death as a welcome, but definite end. The story's tenor is one of political and philosophical skepsis incompatible with Christian belief.

Yet Meyer deliberately leaves the possibility of a Christian interpretation open to the reader. This ambivalence is rooted in his own position comprising a truly modern skepticism as well as a need for security and comfort in traditional religion. Shortly after having completed *Die Versuchung des Pescara* he wrote to Felix Bovet on January 14, 1888: "For in spite of my efforts to escape Christianity ... I feel being led back to it ... regardless of any critical and philosophical knowledge" (*B,* I, 139). Meyer hides his pessimism just as Pescara hides his wound which, in this context, comes to symbolize a deep, incurable loss of hope too frightening to admit openly. And, as in the poems, a balanced form provides the medium which allows and mitigates the expression of disquieting depths.

The comparison between this novella and Meyer's lyric poetry is not accidental. Meyer himself remarked in a letter of November 5, 1887, to Haessel: "Pescara has *little* action and only *one* situation.... [The work] is predominantly lyric" (*W*, XIII, 376). Despite its dramatic structure and its extended dialogues the work has a markedly lyric quality. Not only is there little external action but no real development occurs: all attempts to change things come to naught since Pescara does not respond. Even in the first two chapters, where he does not appear on the scene, his inscrutable personality casts shadows on the feverish activity swirling around him; and once he is on center stage, the unfolding of his situation — more readily discernible to the reader than to his environment — increasingly tinges the story with a melancholy atmosphere. Inner moods are described mostly from an outside point of view by means of endowing objects, details, and colors with specific symbolic significance. Paintings play an important role; often scenic arrangements resemble pictorial compositions — most obviously the end, with Pescara lying dead on the brocade of Sforza's collapsed baldachin — and repeatedly characters sit at a window, framed, so to speak, by its rectangular shape. And since there is almost no progression in the action the symbols that elucidate the situation assume particular weight.

Although *Die Versuchung des Pescara* is not Meyer's last work, it represents an end point. Careful dramatic and symbolic construction creates the most formalized world in all of Meyer's novellas, in a world that impresses us less with a theatrical quality than with shaded colors and modulated tones. In comparison with *Plautus im Nonnenkloster* and *Die Hochzeit des Mönchs,* this picture of the Renaissance is less a dramatic fresco than a finely executed painting. Looking back on Meyer's oeuvre, it is interesting to note that Pescara is in some respects a counterpart of Hutten. Both are hard, experienced fighters and active men, and both are doomed to an early death. But Hutten, though exiled and forsaken, clings to life and hopes for a better future, while Pescara, though famous, respected, and powerful, yearns for death and despairs of life.

III   Angela Borgia

Shortly after the completion of *Pescara,* at the end of 1887,

Meyer fell ill and did not recover until the fall of 1888. He resumed his writing in 1889, but his strength was broken. Soon he abandoned the unwieldy material of *Der Dynast* and returned to the Italian Renaissance and the children of the infamous Pope Alexander Borgia, Lucrezia (1480–1519) and Cesare (1475–1507); the latter had fascinated Meyer as early as the 1840s. Only by straining to the utmost was he able to finish the novella entitled *Angela Borgia* in the summer of 1891. This work is quite different, and while it is lacking in the visual and dramatic concentration so typical for Meyer it elucidates, by its very differences, essential features of his prose writing.

To be sure, there are many familiar elements in this novella which contrasts the beautiful, bewitching Lucrezia Borgia with her younger cousin Angela, showing Lucrezia as having "too little" and Angela "too much conscience" (*W*, XIV, 146). Focusing on the time when Lucrezia was married to Duke Alfonso d'Este of Ferrara, Meyer creates in Alfonso's court another picture of the Renaissance with its beauty and riches blighted by licentiousness and crime. Bacchic life in its extremes is embodied in three figures: in Giulio d'Este, the duke's charming young brother, whose rousing festivities — intended as "classical bacchanalia" — end in "bloodshed and death" (*W*, XIV, 28); in Hercules Strozzi, the young supreme judge of Ferrara who is a total prey to Lucrezia; and in Cesare Borgia whose figure, mingling terror and strange charm, looms in the background. Alfonso's brother, Cardinal Ippolito, represents the shameless politician and churchman who recoils neither from showing his unbridled passion for Angela nor from the hideous crime of having blinded Giulio, whom he sees as his rival. Don Ferrante is the outspoken critic of his brothers, but his flickering spirit only leads him to self-destruction. Duke Alfonso is a rather dry pedant, not given to excesses; but since he needs the cardinal as his political advisor he condones his crime.

Yet this material is treated differently from the earlier works. The dark sides of the Renaissance are much more openly exposed. The men brazenly admit their wild passions, so that the upholding of order often looks like mockery. Therefore, Giulio characterizes his own time as the "century of shameless truth and accomplished lies" (*W*, XIV, 41). While Meyer goes farther than ever in depicting moral degeneration, he also goes farther in establishing positive values. Angela Borgia abhors all irresponsibility; she is unflinching in her adherence to conscience, to right and wrong. Her only flaw lies in an exaggerated severity: extremely conscious of guilt, she sees her life destroyed because twice her innocent remarks precipitated catastrophes — when she praised the beauty of Giulio's eyes, Ippolito had him blinded, and when she admitted her misery, Giulio is prompted to participate in Don Ferrante's conspiracy against the duke, for which he is subsequently sentenced to life imprisonment. Only years later, when the blind prisoner responds to her love does she learn to forgive others and herself. With the help of the Franciscan Father Mamette, Giulio learns to accept his blindness as his spiritual salvation, and in their love Giulio and Angela finally reach a new life rich in inner contentment. Duke Alfonso, too, takes on more positive traits as the story progresses. Even Lucrezia changes for the better once her dangerous brother is dead, and plagued by conscience, the cardinal, on his deathbed, at last asks the duke to pardon Giulio.

On the whole, *Angela Borgia* is characterized by a certain oversimplification. Contrasts are more clearly delineated, and the story develops in such a way as to dissolve the ambivalence present in Lucrezia and Giulio and to offer a solution with unequivocal moral significance. This turn toward definite values was apparently brought about by Meyer's illness, during which he sought comfort in traditional Christian piety. This is mirrored in the fact that neither Ariosto with his poetry nor the philosopher Mirabili bring solace to the blind Giulio, and that only the simple faith of Father Mamette can truly help him. Since Meyer was weakened by his illness and probably exposed to recurring depressions, he needed a stay against his own doubts that had led him earlier to question the traditional values. It even seems as if, with the positive turn of the story, he were trying to stave off a threatening chaos which became all too real in his breakdown of 1892–1893. In a poem written during his internment at Königsfelden and entitled "Der geisteskranke Poet" ("The Deranged Poet") he describes this poet — him-self — as "[having lost all his swords," of being like the pieces of a broken mirror, as "[seeing] everything in double and triple form and [having] lost the truth."⁹

The presentation and style of *Angela Borgia* exhibit some familiar and unfamiliar traits, too. The first chapter, showing Lucrezia's arrival as bride in Ferrara, is another example of Meyer's dense, evocative description. The display of colorful pomp is ironically lighted by Don Ferrante's derogatory remarks as he points out to Angela the cold calculations behind this marriage and the dubious character of politics in general. The chapter has a highly dramatic ending with Giulio's liberation from prison and Angela's ringing verdict on the beautiful youth: "Pity! A thousand pities for you, Don Giulio! Fear God's judgment!" (*W*, XIV, 16). Such density, however, is not kept up, although there are absorbing scenes such as the one preceding the blinding and that of Strozzi's murder. Expressions of contrast so typical for Meyer occur here too: Lucrezia is called a "beautiful misdeed" (*W*, XIV, 104), and the title itself combines the heinous name of Borgia with that of Angela ("angel"). But on the whole there is much less concentration. The story stretches out over about eight years, and repeatedly events are summarized instead of being presented directly or omitted altogether. This results in a relatively continuous overview of the time covered, while in the other novellas involving a longer timespan Meyer focuses on a few crucial moments, leaving the time between unaccounted for. The first two books of *Jürg Jenatsch* are the prime example for this technique, and *Die Versuchung des Pescara* shows the phenomenon on a smaller scale, since the month between the planning of the temptation and its execution is passed over in silence. Many novellas are actually concerned with the events of only a few days — two in *Der Schuss von der Kanzel* and *Plautus im Nonnenkloster*, three in *Die Hochzeit des Mönchs*, five in *Die Richterin* and *Die Versuchung des Pescara*. This highly selective treatment of temporal development, the singling out of a few moments from a much longer timespan, provides Meyer's stories with their particularly clear novella character. In this respect, *Angela Borgia* is much less a novella than the other prose works.

Another feature points in the same direction. In *Angela Borgia* the action falls into two parts, one being concerned with Lucrezia, her infidelity to and deception of Alfonso when her brother calls for her support, the other focusing on Giulio and Angela and the slow, hidden growing of their love. The two lines of action are only externally linked and are presented in separate blocks: Chapters 1, 2, and 9–11 concern Lucrezia; Chapters 3–8 and 12, Giulio and Angela. Such a double action resembles the structure of the novel which, by definition, includes main and secondary actions. In noticing this we also realize how exclusively Meyer, in his other works, limits his attention to one line of action, how consistently he subordinates — in true novella fashion — all details of even such large materials as that encompassed in *Jürg Jenatsch* and *Der Heilige* to the main constellation and dominant problem. *Angela*

Borgia is also the only work where Meyer shows a slow development spread out over a period of time instead of depicting a sudden change, an abrupt surfacing of previously hidden experiences, emotions, or attitudes. Giulio goes through successive stages from exuberant life to deprivation, revolt, and hopeless repentance before he is ready to find new hope in Christian faith and a new, fulfilled life in love. Angela, too, has to traverse a long way from her first veiled emotion that takes the form of a severe judgment of Giulio through hopeless guilt to forgiving love and joyful life. While the two planned novels, *Der Komtur* (*The Commander,* sketched out in the late 1870s) and *Der Dynast,* never grew beyond some meager beginnings,[10] *Angela Borgia* represents Meyer's most serious try at a novel. It remains an attempt, however, since the work is too short and too concise for a full-fledged novel.

In judging this last work it is, therefore, not enough just to note its lack of concentration. Rather we should see the somewhat problematic nature of *Angela Borgia* in the larger context of Meyer's style and attitudes. *Die Versuchung des Pescara* constitutes an extreme: fixed pictorial compositions and a richly elaborate symbolism dominate this most static of Meyer's works. It is thus no wonder that Meyer remarked to Hermann Lingg in 1890: "I have a beautiful subject but would like to treat it in a new manner" (*W,* XIV, 143). Indeed, *Angela Borgia* reveals a new attention to development, a step toward the broad richness (*Fülle*) which Meyer often — and rightly — recognized as alien to him, but which he nevertheless coveted because it was an essential element of the poet's image as the time saw it. Thus, by trying to move in the direction of a broader novelistic work he conforms more to the traditional concepts of prose writing. On the philosophical level, too, he retreated from his position of probing skepticism and turned to a more positive vision. In this context, it is significant that he starts with the same material as in the earlier works, the questionable and ambivalent Renaissance, but is determined to show its potential for a positive development. In a letter to Frey of August 12, 1891, he wrote: "...Angela Borgia [is] completed, [it is] if not a work of art, still a vigorous act of volition" (*W,* XIV, 155). This designation of the work as an "act of volition" is usually applied only to the strain needed to finish it, but the term can also be applied to Meyer's determination to write a positive work. In an almost Utopian fashion he constructs a development that changes a violent, shameless world into one of growing responsibility and deepening love and that ends with the idyllic vision of Angela's and Giulio's happiness. In other words, Meyer returned to a more traditional attitude that places horrors and anxieties into a clearly moral framework.

If we should be disappointed by this turn to conventionality, we should not forget that new depressions were casting their shadows on Meyer. Forty years earlier depressions had led him to depths that the mature artist could transform into a fascinating, ambiguous world probing, as it were, into the darkness and hidden wounds of his own seemingly vital era.

CHAPTER 9

Style of Ambivalence —
Convention and Modernity

A GAIN and again we have seen Meyer as a transitional figure standing between acceptance and rejection of the conventions of his time. This position is also reflected in his style, in his aim for the conventional literary forms that he either adapts to his own unconventional purposes or does not use at all. The form most dependent on tradition is the drama: in the later nineteenth century it was still valued as the highest form of literature, and Meyer aspired throughout his life to prove himself as a dramatic writer. He never succeeded, and this failure elucidates, in yet another way, the peculiarities of his style.

Dramas were among the first projects of the young Meyer in the 1840s;[1] and later, during his work with larger historical materials, his desire to write plays was revived. In his letters, he mentions dramatic plans often and with such confidence that we are surprised to see the meager results of his dramatic attempts. There exist a scenario and a short scene for a Jenatsch drama (*W,* X, 297–300), three outlines and six scenes for a play about Frederick II and Petrus Vinea,[2] and ten fragmentary scenes for a stage work about Angela Borgia (*W,* XIV, 188–206). The projects for dramas about Gustav Adolf, the wedded monk, and the judge seem to have existed only in his imagination.[3] While Gottfried Keller experienced the same frustrated desire to write dramas, Meyer's case is even more intriguing because his novellas have such a pronounced dramatic quality that they provide excellent illustrations for Theodor Storm's definition of the novella as "the sister of the drama." Upon closer examination of Meyer's dramatic fragments, however, Hans Corrodi concludes that Meyer is basically a lyric writer who,

153

unable to identify directly with his figures, presents his stories in indirect ways. Corrodi also emphasizes that Meyer's strikingly visual images and scenes depend largely on atmospheric description and are pervaded by a deep melancholy.[4] In agreement with Corrodi is Georges Brunet, who adds that Meyer was exposed to such an intense personal drama that he sought to portray conciliation rather than direct confrontation.[5] Yet in a larger perspective, Meyer's unsuccessful dramatic ambition is a manifestation of his transitional stance. The drama he envisaged — a historical one in the tradition of Schiller — demonstrated the conventions of his time: it contained figures of heroic deeds and passions and it portrayed fervent life and momentous decisions, all of which were designed to arouse admiration and to offer some lesson in moral principles. In addition, the dramatist illustrated in a most spectacular way his creative powers by compressing vast material into a relatively short space and by inspiring entire audiences with suspense and pathos. For Meyer, as well as for his period, the successful dramatist represented the exemplary writer dominating a rich world of thoughts and emotions. This kind of genius was best represented by Richard Wagner, whom Meyer regarded as requiring "the most attentive consideration as an important part of our era, that is, of ourselves" (in a letter to L. von François of June 16, 1883). In these respects, Meyer is a representative of his time, the *Gründerzeit* ("Founders' Era") when the political and economical prosperity of Germany favored admiration of greatness and power, adherence to conventional morality, and conservative attitudes in general.

Meyer, however, could only long for such a world of force, activity, and order, a world which he had already left behind. In his novellas he preserves its heroic settings, but he takes a skeptical view of the heroes and their deeds by showing that their high principles might be rooted in questionable psychological motives. Thus, conventional values appear in a dubious light: behind Schadau's religious fervor there is smug self-righteousness; behind Jenatsch's patriotism a boundless lust for power; behind Astorre's mercy a sexual desire; and behind Pescara's loyalty an almost nihilistic despair. Again and again Meyer's stories end with death, but instead of signifying a final moral triumph, death, for this author, symbolizes the hopelessness of a situation. Constructive reconciliation between Henry II and Becket has become impossible; Gustel Leubelfing cannot find an appropriate place for herself; and Astorre's and Antiope's love cannot survive in the everyday world.

Highly ironic as well is the death of Julian Boufflers: his hallucinatory death for the king is a delusion in both the literal and figurative sense since the king, and shown in the novella, does not represent principles worth dying for.

In Meyer's novellas conventional concepts are thus intertwined with more modern insights; but in his typical manner Meyer avoids taking a decisive stance. Instead he presents his stories from different perspectives, deliberately foregoing direct authorial comments. Therefore, it is possible for readers to view him as an advocate of conventional moral and religious attitudes. Thus Schadau's and Becket's stories, for example, have substantial religious significance, and Pescara can be seen as a model of loyalty. Yet the reader who penetrates further into Meyer's world will piece together the different perspectives and, noticing the author's subtle intimations, will realize that behind the conventional facade of this world there is surprising depth and insight of a far more modern nature. From such a point of view, Jenatsch, while not entirely excusable, can be seen as the product of his time, Astorre as the victim of repressions and warped conventional attitudes. The stories of Stemma and Pescara likewise show that justice and loyalty do not necessarily constitute such clearly ethical acts as is commonly assumed. What appears at first as a clear moral order, or even a meaningful divine plan, reveals itself, upon closer examination, as an amalgam of propositions ranging from blind, incomprehensible fate to an explanation of fate based upon psychological reactions.

It was not Meyer's purpose to demonstrate a definitive view of the world. Rather, he intended to unveil the often confusing complexities that lie behind and beneath the established conventions of interpreting life and human nature. By using allusions, irony, and changing perspectives, by avoiding direct comments and omniscient stance Meyer undermines the traditional concepts and opens the reader's eyes to the many hidden motives that shape human life. As Klaus Jesiorkowski shows in his article,[6] Meyer practices a *Kunst der Perspektive,* a perspectival art devoid of a uniform, or even a clearly prevailing point of view. Although inherent in all of Meyer's prose works, this narrative relativism is most obvious in the framework stories, and especially in *Der Heilige* and *Die Hochzeit des Mönchs.* With his narrators, Meyer formulates his concept of the writer who has lost his omniscience in a complex world and "must acquiesce in limited insights, even in uncertainty and doubts."[7]

It is typical for Meyer that he remained basically within traditional forms, yet adapted them step by step to his own untraditional purposes, thus changing them from within rather than from without. This type of slow empirical procedure especially characterizes his poetry. There he started with the traditional content and form of romantic confessional poetry (*Erlebnisdichtung*), but as he gradually moved toward objective description of static images and isolated motifs he found a means of infusing conventional metrical forms with a new, subdued lyricism. In the context of German literature of the 1870s and 1880s, the resulting symbolist poems are as unconventional as Meyer's way of writing them. By separating and recombining images, symbolic elements, by transposing stanzas from one poem to another, Meyer practiced what Baudelaire saw as the task of modern art, namely, to decompose reality and to reassemble its separate elements into works of art. This aspect of Meyer's poetry is visible mainly in the development of his lyrics and in the few poems in which he reveals his poetic principle.[8] The finished poems, however, present unified images. This, too, reflects Meyer's situation: the modern process of decomposing and recomposing takes place behind the facade of a seemingly intact world. Similarly, in the novellas the conventional values are preserved on one level while on another they are being closely scrutinized and decomposed. Unlike Baudelaire and Nietzsche, Meyer was unable to attack the conventions of his time openly. In order to voice his criticism and his disturbing insights, he needed the protective frame of his bourgeois everyday existence and the guise of moral interpretations for his works.

Form appears as the main defense against a threatening disintegration of the world. For it is striking how often Meyer uses narrative structures that are symmetrical, even cyclic, to produce the impression of order and coherence. The most obvious examples are the structures of *Huttens letzte Tage, Plautus im Nonnenkloster, Die Versuchung des Pescara,* and of the *Gedichte.* Among the poems there are many instances of such cyclic forms on a smaller scale as, for example, in "Der römische Brunnen" and "Schwarzschattende Kastanie." Yet for the attentive reader such structures cannot and should not provide real contentment; rather they emphasize the underlying vision of a complex and unsettling world that is on the verge of disintegrating.

Because of the experiences leading to his breakdown in 1852, and because of his existence within a society that held fast to conventions in reaction to a rapidly changing world, Meyer was bound to develop an ambivalent attitude in his longing for security while perceiving its pitfalls. Consequently, his poetic world is equivocal and his style had to be attuned to portraying a double-faced world, to addressing his bourgeois readers in the terms of his times as well as to unveiling the hidden depths of a decaying age, to hinting at the abyss behind the well-ordered surface. And this, in turn, corresponds to Meyer's transitional position between the *Gründerzeit* with its traditional values and the modern insights that show him to be allied with symbolist art and with the relativistic, psychological view of morality and truth proposed by Nietzsche. Meyer's work is significant for its very ambivalence, for it shows us the values of the later nineteenth century and their dubious background. Thus it is not surprising that he admired and befriended the writers around Paul Heyse in the Munich Circle (*Münchner Dichterkreis*), who represented the *Gründerzeit,* while also being attracted to Dostoevski, Ibsen, and Hauptmann.[9]

Using conventional forms Meyer nevertheless is a modern writer. His innovations do not immediately strike the eye, but at closer reading they become apparent and certainly connect him with the modern currents of his period. Though a recluse in Kilchberg and an outsider on the contemporary literary scene, Meyer still felt the pulse of his time by creating a singular vision of modern complexities in a historical guise.

Notes and References

Chapter One

1. In the Great Council the city with its 10,000 inhabitants had 130 representatives, the canton with its 200,000 inhabitants only 82; 8 of the high bailiffs for the Canton came from the city, as did 140 of the 160 protestant ministers. See S. Zurlinden, *Hundert Jahre: Bilder aus der Geschichte der Stadt Zürich in der Zeit von 1814–1914* (Zurich: Berichthaus, 1915), I, 65; Wilhelm Oechsli, *History of Switzerland,* trans. Eden Paul and Cedar Paul (Cambridge: Cambridge University Press, 1922), p. 317. For a short historical account of this period see Edgar Bonjour, *A Short History of Switzerland,* trans. H. S. Offler and G. R. Potter (Oxford: Oxford University Press, Clarendon Press, 1952), pp. 251–56.

2. Betsy Meyer, *Conrad Ferdinand Meyer: In der Erinnerung seiner Schwester* (Berlin: Paetel, 1903), p. 55; hereafter referred to as *Erinnerung.*

3. Konrad Meyer (1824–1903) wrote mostly dialect poems; he is now forgotten except for the fact that he caused the other Conrad Meyer to change his name.

4. Meyer, *Erinnerung,* p. 81.

5. Ibid., p. 56.

6. The study was published in 1836 and drew praise from the great German historian Leopold von Ranke. Ferdinand Meyer also wrote a lengthy article about the abortive attempt to secularize the bishopric in Chur in 1551–1561; see Adolf Frey, *Conrad Ferdinand Meyer: Sein Leben und seine Werke,* 4th ed. (Stuttgart: Cotta, 1925), pp. 14–15, hereafter referred to as *Meyer. See also p. 69.*

7. See Isidor Sadger, *Konrad Ferdinand Meyer: Eine pathographisch-psychologische Studie* (Wiesbaden: Bergemann, 1908), pp. 7–8.

8. See Arthur Kielholz "Conrad Ferdinand Meyer und seine Beziehungen zu Königsfelden" *Monatsschrift für Psychologie und Neurologie* 109 (1944), 260–61.

9. Betsy later copied and preserved these poems, some of which are dated between 1839 and 1846. The same folder in the C. F. Meyer Archives in the Zentralbibliothek in Zurich (CFM 178) also contains a few poems in Meyer's own writing apparently belonging to the same period.

10. Gustav Pfizer (1807–1890) was a well-known poet during his life-

time, but is now forgotten. Meyer's mother had met and befriended his wife in the 1830s.

11. Only a few passages from these poems have so far been published; the completion of the historical-critical Meyer edition in the near future will make these poems available and allow a detailed analysis.

12. Meyer, *Erinnerung,* pp. 93–94.

13. Ibid., p. 95.

14. Letter to Alfred Meissner of April 14, 1877; see Adolf Frey, ed., *Briefe Conrad Ferdinand Meyers nebst seinen Rezensionen und Aufsätzen,* 2 vols. (Leipzig: Haessel, 1908), II, 270. Hereafter cited in the text as *B.*

15. See Karl Fehr, *Conrad Ferdinand Meyer,* Sammlung Metzler, vol. 102 (Stuttgart: Metzler, 1971), p. 24, and Alfred Zäch, *Conrad Ferdinand Meyer: Dichtkunst als Befreiung aus Lebenshemmnissen,* Wirkung und Gestalt, vol. 12 (Frauenfeld: Huber, 1973), p. 18.

16. Meyer, *Erinnerung,* p. 95.

17. Frey, *Meyer,* p. 52.

18. For a detailed discussion of this point see George W. Reinhardt, "The Political Views of the Young Conrad Ferdinand Meyer: With a Note on *Das Amulett,*" *German Quarterly* 45 (1972), 270–94.

19. Meyer, *Erinnerung,* pp. 97–98.

20. Ibid., pp. 102–3.

21. Robert d'Harcourt, *C.-F. Meyer: La Crise de 1852–1856: Lettres de C.-F. Meyer et de son entourage* (Paris: Alcan 1913), hereafter cited in the text as *C.*

22. Hans Günther Bressler in his article "Gedichte aus C. F. Meyers Spätkrankheit," *Monatsschrift für Psychiatrie und Neurologie* 125 (1953), 320–28, mentions several possible definitions; Arthur Kielholz (see footnote 8 above) concludes that Meyer's artistic personality defies every psychiatric pattern.

23. Louis Vulliemin (1797–1879) translated Johannes von Müller's *Geschichten der Schweizerischen Eidgenossenschaft* into French; he continued Müller's work by writing the volumes dealing with the sixteenth, seventeenth, and early eighteenth centuries; Vulliemin also wrote a *History of the Swiss Confederation.*

24. This translation is now easily accessible in the following modern edition: Augustin Thierry, *Erzählungen aus den merowingischen Zeiten. Aus dem Französischen übersetzt von Conrad Ferdinand Meyer,* ed. Gerlinde Bretzigheimer and Hans Zeller (Zurich: Manesse, 1972).

25. This translation was published by Beyel in Zurich, but because of the publisher's sudden death most copies were destroyed.

26. Frey, *Meyer,* p. 71.

27. Ibid., p. 104.

28. Ibid., pp. 110 and 108.

29. Ibid., p. 126.

30. To Julius Rodenberg, April 21, 1880; see August Langmesser, ed., *Conrad Ferdinand Meyer und Julius Rodenberg: Ein Briefwechsel* (Berlin: Paetel, 1918), p. 66.

31. See Adolf Frey, ed., *Conrad Ferdinand Meyers Briefe nebst seinen Rezensionen und Aufsätzen,* II, 520.

32. This letter was only recently found and published by Alfred Zäch in the *Literaturbeilage der Neuen Zürcher Zeitung,* no. 517 (November 5, 1972), 49–50.

33. New York: Columbia University Press, 1936.

34. See also p. 106–7

35. The translation was subsequently done by Betsy; Meyer only translated the passages taken from the works of French poets and wrote a short introduction for the volume entitled *Der himmlische Vater: Sieben Reden von Ernst Naville* (Leipzig: Haessel, 1865).

36. Anton Reitler, *Eine literarische Skizze zu des Dichters 60. Geburtstag* (Leipzig, 1885), quoted in Conrad Ferdinand Meyer, *Sämtliche Werke: Historisch-kritische Ausgabe,* ed. Hans Zeller and Alfred Zäch (Bern: Benteli, 1958–), VIII, 150. Of the 15 planned volumes of this edition four — volumes 5–7, and 15 — have not yet appeared; references to this edition will be cited in the text as *W.* Where possible the chapters are also indicated, so that the passage can be more easily located in a different edition.

37. "Conrad Ferdinand Meyer, *Huttens letzte Tage* and the Liberal Ideal," *Oxford German Studies,* no. 5, (1970), pp. 67–89.

38. This poem, dated July 13, 1875, is published in Constanze Speyer, ed., *Gedichte an seine Braut* (Zurich: Oprecht, 1940), p. 31.

39. Three paintings — a view from Corsica toward Elba, Meyer's home in Kilchberg, and the Ziegler castle in Steinegg near the Lake of Constance — were inherited by my family, since Luise Ziegler's sister Henriette had married my great-grandfather Diethelm Burkhard, who was a protestant minister in Küsnacht.

40. Unpublished letter dated December 3, 1884; quoted in Zäch, *Conrad Ferdinand Meyer, p.* 41.

41. The institution founded and directed by Samuel Zeller was located in Männedorf on the Lake of Zurich. Betsy bought a house there in which she supervised lighter cases until 1892; see below p. 164, footnote 3.

42. See footnote 8.

43. See footnote 22.

44. See Alfred Zäch, "Unbekannte Gedichte C. F. Meyers aus seinen letzten Jahren" *Literaturbeilage der Neuen Zürcher Zeitung,* no. 301, (November 4, 1973), 49.

Chapter Two

1. Betsy Meyer, *Erinnerung,* pp. 56–57.

2. Meyer's few references to Nietzsche can be found in the following letters: to L. von François of October 15, 1888, in Anton Bettelheim, ed., *Louise von François und Conrad Ferdinand Meyer: Ein Briefwechsel,* 2d ed. (Berlin: Vereinigung wissenschaftlicher Verleger, 1920), p. 235 and Appendix C, pp. 304–5; and to François Wille of November 30, 1887, and December 12, 1888. The question of Meyer's knowledge of Nietzsche is discussed in detail by W. P. Bridgwater, "C. F. Meyer and Nietzsche," *Modern Language Review* 60 (1965), 568–83.

3. See pp. 21–22 and 29–30.

4. Meyer, *Erinnerung,* p. 163.

5. Title of the first chapter in Heinrich Henel's book *The Poetry of Conrad Ferdinand Meyer* (Madison: University of Wisconsin Press, 1954).

6. This edition is published in the series Dichtung und Wirklichkeit, Ullstein-Buch, no. 5028 (Frankfurt, 1965).

Chapter Three

1. See *W,* VIII, 201.

2. In this essay, which was not written until 1890, Meyer designates the 1870 poem as the first one; evidently he forgot the one of 1866.

3. Until recently a detailed analysis of the form in *Hutten* was lacking. See my article "Die Entdeckung der Form in *Huttens letzte Tage,*" *Archiv für das Studium der neueren Sprachen und Literaturen* 209 (1972–1973), 259–72.

4. See pp. 33–34.

5. For decades, editors considered the tenth edition of 1896 as representative, yet the changes appearing in the ninth and tenth editions (1894–1896) are not Meyer's but Betsy's (see *W,* VIII, 225f).

6. See *W,* VIII, 520–34.

7. See *W,* VIII, 456–58.

8. "Conrad Ferdinand Meyers Dichtung *Engelberg* und die Verserzählung des 19. Jahrhunderts," in *134. Neujahrsblatt zum Besten des Waisenhauses Zürich für 1971* (Zurich: Beer, 1971).

9. See p. 125–26.

Chapter Four

1. See "C. F. Meyers Beziehungen zu Königsfelden," p. 270.

2. See David A. Jackson, "Schadau, the Satirized Narrator, in C. F. Meyer's *Das Amulett,*" *Trivium* 7 (1972), 61–69; Paul Schimmelpfennig, "C. F. Meyer's Religion of the Heart: A Reevaluation of *Das Amulett,*" *Germanic Review* 47 (1972), 181–202. The latter article also contains a concise survey of critical comments on pp. 181–82.

3. Alfred Zäch, in the historical-critical edition, surmises that Mérimée's influence is to be seen in terms of plot only (*W,* XI, 226).

4. See *Conrad Ferdinand Meyer in Selbstzeugnissen und Bilddokumenten.* (Hamburg: Rowohlt, 1975), p. 79.

5. See footnote 2.

6. To J. R. Rahn Meyer wrote on January 18, 1872, that Jenatsch "had been in [his] head for nearly ten years" (*B*, I, 232). Serious work on the project, however, did not start until 1866.

7. Simple page references will apply to this tenth volume of the historical-critical edition.

8. "Conrad Ferdinand Meyer und die Grösse," in *Unbehagen im Kleinstaat* (Zurich: Artemis, 1963), pp. 19–22.

9. See Keller's letters to Paul Heyse of December 26, 1876, and to Theodor Storm of January 5, 1883 and June 9, 1884.

10. See *Conrad Ferdinand Meyer in Selbstzeugnissen,* p. 82.

11. Valentin Herzog, *Ironische Erzählformen bei Conrad Ferdinand Meyer dargestellt am Jürg Jenatsch,* Basler Studien zur deutschen Sprache und Literatur, vol. 42 (Bern: Francke, 1970).

12. "Ueber das Zeitgerüst des Erzählens am Beispiel des *Jürg Jenatsch,*" *Deutsche Vierteljahresschrift für Literaturwissenschaft und Geistesgeschichte* 24 (1950), 1–32.

13. See pp. 38–40.

14. Alfred Zäch, *Conrad Ferdinand Meyer,* p. 139.

15. "The Ambiguous Explosion: C. F. Meyer's *Der Schuss von der Kanzel,*" *German Quarterly* 43 (1970), 213.

Chapter Five

1. For a discussion of the sources see Alfred Zäch's remarks in Volume 13 of the historical-critical edition (pp. 301–5), and Richard Travis Hardaway, "Conrad Ferdinand Meyer's *Der Heilige* in Relation to Its Sources," *Publications of the Modern Language Association* 58 (1943), 245–63.

2. See *W*, XIII, 284–85; only the first three chapters are preserved (*W*, XIII, 305–22). In the following, simple page numbers refer to Volume 13 of the historical-critical edition.

3. See above p. 48.

4. See *Realism and Reality: Studies in the German Novella of Poetic Realism,* (Chapel Hill: University of North Carolina Press, 1954), p. 107.

5. "Zur Funktion der Gnade-Episode in C. F. Meyers *Der Heilige*" in *Lebendige Form: Festschrift für Heinrich Henel,* ed. Jeffrey L. Sammons and Ernst Schürer (Munich: W. Fink, 1970), pp. 249–51.

6. W. A. Coupe, "Thierry, Meyer and *Der Heilige,*" *German Life and Letters,* n.s. 16 (1962–1963), 113–15.

7. Colin Walker, "Unbelief and Martyrdom in C. F. Meyer's *Der Heilige,*" *German Life and Letters,* n.s. 21 (1967–1968), 120.

8. Lewis W. Tusken, "C. F. Meyer's *Der Heilige:* The Problem of

Becket's Conversion," *Seminar* 7 (1971), 214–15.

9. The closeness of Meyer's thinking to that of Nietzsche is also borne out by Heinz Wetzel in his article "Der allzumenschliche Heilige: C. F. Meyers Novelle im Lichte von Nietzsches Gedanken zur Genealogie der Moral," *Etudes Germaniques* 30 (1975), 204–19.

Chapter Six

1. This estimate is based on the material available in Volumes 2–4 of the historical-critical edition, covering the first seven of the nine cycles in *Gedichte*.

2. For this reason, there are few manuscripts for poems written after 1879 when Betsy ceased to act as secretary.

3. (Madison: University of Wisconsin Press, 1954), p. 139; hereafter referred to as *Poetry*.

4. Meyer's interest in French literature — strongest in the 1840s and 1850s — was always mainly directed toward classical and romantic works.

5. See Heinrich Henel on "Lethe," "Stapfen," and "Das Seelchen"; Emil Staiger on "Die tote Liebe"; Beatrice Sandberg-Braun on "Lieder-seelen," "Schwüle," and "Nachtgeräusche"; and Gustav Beckers on "Der verwundete Baum." See also the bibliography.

6. See "Lyrik der Beschaulichkeit," *Monatshefte* 60 (1968), p. 227.

7. "Linguistic Patterns, Literary Structure, and the Genesis of 'Der römische Brunnen,' " *Language and Style* 4 (1971), 83–115; the article also contains an extensive bibliography.

8. For a thorough discussion of the differences between romantic and symbolist poetry see Heinrich Henel, "Erlebnisdichtung und Symbolismus," *Deutsche Vierteljahrsschrift für Literaturwissenschaft und Geistesgeschichte* 32 (1958), especially pp. 82–85, and Emil Staiger, "Das Spätboot," in *Die Kunst der Interpretation* (Zurich: Atlantis, 1955), pp. 254–56.

9. See above p. 60–61.

10. See also p. 54. The poem "Tag, schein herein, und Leben, flieh hinaus" is another case in point: in the last version Meyer changes the middle stanza so as to describe his youth when he was "stifled in a dream." This change creates a moving contrast to the hope and brightness expressed in the first and third stanzas (*W,* III, 161–64).

11. Lena F. Dahme in *Women in the Life and Art of C. F. Meyer* attributes "Weihgeschenk" and "Der Blutstropfen" to Constance von Rodt, "Stapfen," "Wetterleuchten," "Lethe," and "Einer Toten" to Clelia Weydmann. Yet the death motif in "Lethe" is alrady present in the first version of 1860, years before Clelia died, while the death motif in "Stapfen" is not developed until the very last version of 1881–1882.

12. See Heinrich Henel, "Conrad Ferdinand Meyer: 'Lethe,' " in

Benno von Wiese, ed., *Die deutsche Lyrik,* 2 vols. (Dusseldorf: Bagel 1957), II, 222.

13. See Emil Staiger, "Das Spätboot," p. 273.

14. See also Betty Loeffler Fletcher, "The Supreme Moment as a Motif in C. F. Meyer's Poems," *Monatshefte* 42 (1950), 27–32, and my dissertation *C. F. Meyer und die antike Mythologie,* Zürcher Beiträge zur deutschen Literatur- und Geistesgeschichte, vol. 25 (Zurich: Atlantis 1966), especially the chapters "Der trunkene Gott" and "Traumbesitz."

15. Quoted in Anna Balakian, *The Symbolist Movement* (New York: Random House, 1967), p. 87.

16. Vienna: W. Braumüller, 1918.

17. See Henel, *Poetry,* pp. 245–52.

18. See "Salon de 1859," part III, "La reine des facultés," in *Oeuvres Complètes* (Paris: Gallimard, 1961), pp. 1037–38.

Chapter Seven

1. The new translations of Meyer's complete prose works by George F. Folkers, David D. Dickens, and Marion W. Sonnenfeld slightly differ in two of these titles: *Plautus in the Convent* and *A Boy Suffers.*

2. See "Conrad Ferdinand Meyer und die Grösse," p. 34.

3. Quoted in Maria Nils, *Betsy. Die Schwester Conrad Ferdinand Meyers* (Frauenfeld: Huber, 1943), p. 216.

4. See Henel, *Poetry,* pp. 119–25.

5. See Jackson, *Conrad Ferdinand Meyer,* p. 105. Although Ferdinand Meyer had a potential for understanding his son, he probably realized it only on rare occasions in his brief life, such as in the two hiking trips of 1836 and 1838; see p. 15.

6. *The Stories of C. F. Meyer* (Oxford: Oxford University Press, Clarendon Press, 1962), pp. 73–74. Williams' suggestions are further developed by Martin Swales in his article "Fagon's Defeat: Some Remarks on C. F. Meyer's *Das Leiden eines Knaben,*" *Germanic Review* 52 (1977), 29–43.

7. In a rudimentary way Meyer asks his readers to do what later Brecht does, that is, asks them to judge for themselves, to take a critical look at the presented material and not to accept a judgment already made.

8. See Benno von Wiese, "Conrad Ferdinand Meyer: *Die Hochzeit des Mönchs,*" in *Die deutsche Novelle von Goethe bis Kafka* (Düsseldorf: Bagel, 1964), II, 190.

9. Williams, *The Stories of C. F. Meyer,* pp. 111–12.

10. *Deutsche Literatur im bürgerlichen Realismus,* 2d ed. (Stuttgart: Metzler, 1964), pp. 836–37.

11. Michael Shaw, "C. F. Meyer's Resolute Heroes," *Deutsche Vierteljahresschrift für Literaturwissenschaft und Geistesgeschichte* 40 (1966), 372–81. This article also contains a useful survey of interpretations.

12. David A. Jackson, "Dante the Dupe in *Die Hochzeit des Mönchs*," *German Life and Letters*, n.s. 25 (1971), 5–15.

13. Novalis, *Fragmente* I, ed. Ewald Wachsmuth (Heidelberg: L. Schneider, 1957), "Enzyklopädie IV," no. 1366, p. 365.

14. Ernst Feise, "*Die Hochzeit des Mönchs* von Conrad Ferdinand Meyer: Eine Formanalyse," in *Xenion: Themes, Forms and Ideas in German Literature* (Baltimore: Johns Hopkins Press, 1950), p. 224.

Chapter Eight

1. In the new translation the title reads *Pescara's Temptation*.

2. See letter to L. von François of February 22, 1885; see also David A. Jackson, *Conrad Ferdinand Meyer*, pp. 109–10, and "C. F. Meyer's *Die Richterin*: A Tussle with Tolstoi?" *Trivium* 9 (1974), 39–49.

3. See especially W. D. Williams, *The Stories of C. F. Meyer*, p. 116.

4. See Frederick J. Beharriell, "C. F. Meyer and the Origins of Psychoanalysis," *Monatshefte* 47 (1955), 140–48. Freud's essay on *Die Richterin* is printed in *The Origins of Psycho-Analysis: Letters to Wilhelm Fliess, Drafts and Notes 1887–1902*, ed. Marie Bonaparte, Anna Freud, and Ernst Kris, trans. Eric Mosbacher and James Strachey (New York: Basic Books, 1954), pp. 256–57.

5. See *Origins of Psycho-Analysis*, p. 270.

6. See Jacques Arouet, "*Die Versuchung des Pescara*. A Justification of Its Title," *Journal of English and Germanic Philology* 45 (1946), 240–43.

7. See "C. F. Meyer's Resolute Heroes," p. 390; a discussion of several interpretations can be found on p. 382.

8. See Shaw, "C. F. Meyer's Resolute Heroes," p. 388.

9. Quoted in Hans-Günther Bressler, "Gedichte aus C. F. Meyers Spätkrankheit," p. 321.

10. See Adolf Frey, ed., *Conrad Ferdinand Meyers unvollendete Prosadichtungen*, 2 vols. (Leipzig: Haessel, 1916).

Chapter Nine

1. See p. 20.

2. See Frey, *Conrad Ferdinand Meyers unvollendete Prosadichtungen*, I, 176–81, 189–92.

3. While Meyer used to discard manuscripts of finished works, it seems unlikely that he should have destroyed a considerable number of dramatic manuscripts relating to unfinished dramas.

4. *Conrad Ferdinand Meyer und sein Verhältnis zum Drama* (Leipzig: Hesse and Becker, 1922), pp. 117–20.

5. See *C. F. Meyer et la nouvelle*, Germanica, vol. 10 (Paris: Didier, (967).

6. "Die Kunst der Perspektive: Zur Epik Conrad Ferdinand Meyers," *Germanisch-romanische Monatsschrift,* n.s. 17 (1967), 398–416.

7. Jesiorkowski, "Die Kunst der Perspektive," p. 401.

8. See pp. 60–61, 100–101, 120–22.

9. See letters to François Wille of March 30, 1883 and January 16, 1891; to F. von Wyss of October 19, 1889; and to Carl Spitteler of February 9, 1892.

Selected Bibliography

PRIMARY SOURCES

1. Collected Works

Sämtliche Werke. Historisch-kritische Ausgabe. Edited by Alfred Zäch and Hans Zeller (Bern: Benteli, 1958–). Volumes 5–7 and 15 have not yet appeared.

"*Clara,* Novelle von Conrad Ferdinand Meyer." Edited by Constanze Speyer. *Corona* 8 (1938), 395–416.

Conrad Ferdinand Meyers unvollendete Prosadichtungen. Edited by Adolf Frey (Leipzig: Haessel, 1916). 2 vols.

Gedichte an seine Braut. Edited by Constanze Speyer (Zurich: Oprecht, 1940).

2. Collections of letters and recollections

BETTELHEIM, ANTON, ed. *Louise von François und Conrad Ferdinand Meyer: Ein Briefwechsel* (Berlin: Reimer, 1905; rev. ed., Berlin: Vereinigung wissenschaftlicher Verleger, 1920).

Frey, Adolf, ed. *Briefe Conrad Ferdinand Meyers nebst seinen Rezensionen und Aufsätzen.* 2 vols. (Leipzig: Haessel, 1908).

D'HARCOURT, ROBERT, *C.-F. Meyer: La Crise de 1852–1856. Lettres de C.-F. Meyer et de son entourage* (Paris: Alcan, 1913).

LANGMESSER, AUGUST, ed. *Conrad Ferdinand Meyer und Julius Rodenberg: Ein Briefwechsel* (Berlin: Paetel, 1918).

MEYER, BETSY, *Conrad Ferdinand Meyer in der Erinnerung seiner Schwester* (Berlin: Paetel, 1903).

ZELLER, HANS, ed., "Frau Anna von Doss über Conrad Ferdinand Meyer. Berichte und Briefe." *Euphorion* 57 (1963), 390–410.

3. Translations

FOLKERS, GEORGE F., DICKENS, DAVID B., and SONNENFELD, MARION W. *The Complete Narrative Prose of Conrad Ferdinand Meyer* (Lewisburg: Bucknell University Press, 1976). 2 vols.

SECONDARY SOURCES

AROUET, JACQUES, "*Die Versuchung des Pescara.* A Justification of

Its Title." *Journal of English and Germanic Philology* 45 (1946), 440–43.

BAUMGARTEN, FRANZ FERDINAND. *Das Werk Conrad Ferdinand Meyers: Renaissance-Empfinden und Stilkunst* (Munich: Beck, 1917).

BECKERS, GUSTAV. "Morone und Pescara. Proteisches Verwandlungsspiel und existentielle Metamorphose. Ein Beitrag zur Interpretation von C. F. Meyers Novelle *Die Versuchung des Pescara*." *Euphorion* 63 (1969), 117–45.

_____. "Der verwundete Baum. Infrastrukturelle Analyse zum genetischen Typus lyrischer Arbeit bei Conrad Ferdinand Meyer." *Colloquia Germanica* (1973), 257–312.

BEHARRIELL, FREDERICK J. "C. F. Meyer and the Origins of Psychoanalysis." *Monatshefte* 47 (1955), 140–48.

BRESSLER, HANS-GÜNTHER. "Gedichte aus C. F. Meyers Spätkrankheit." *Monatsschrift für Psychiatrie und Neurologie* 125 (1953), 320–28.

BRUNET, GEORGES. *C. F. Meyer et la nouvelle,* Germanica, vol. 10 (Paris: Didier, 1967).

BURKHARD, ARTHUR. *Conrad Ferdinand Meyer: The Style and the Man* (Cambridge: Harvard University Press, 1932).

BURKHARD, MARIANNE. *C. F. Meyer und die antike Mythologie.* Zürcher Beiträge zur deutschen Literatur-und Geistesgeschichte, vol. 25 (Zurich: Atlantis, 1966).

_____. "Bacchus Biformis. Zu einem Motiv im Werk C. F. Meyers." *Neophilologus* 55 (1971), 418–32.

_____. "Zeit und Raum im Werk C. F. Meyers." *German Quarterly* 44 (1971), 331–40.

_____. "Die Entdeckung der Form in *Huttens letzte Tage*." *Archiv für das Studium der neueren Sprachen und Literaturen* 209 (1972–1973), 259–72.

CORRODI, HANS. *Conrad Ferdinand Meyer und sein Verhältnis zum Drama* (Leipzig: Hesse and Becker, 1922).

COUPE, W. A. "Thierry, Meyer and *Der Heilige*." *German Life and Letters,* n.s. 16 (1962–1963), 105–16.

CRICHTON, MARY C. "Zur Funktion der Gnade-Episode in C. F. Meyers *Der Heilige*." In *Lebendige Form: Festschrift für Heinrich Henel,* edited by Jeffrey Sammons and Ernst Schürer, pp. 245–58 (Munich: Fink, 1970).

DAHME, LENA F. *Women in the Life and Art of Conrad Ferdinand Meyer* (New York: Columbia University Press, 1936).

FAESI, ROBERT. *Conrad Ferdinand Meyer,* Sammlung Die Schweiz im deutschen Geistesleben, vol. 36 (Leipzig: Haessel, 1924).

FEHR, KARL. *Conrad Ferdinand Meyer,* Sammlung Metzler, vol. 102 (Stuttgart: Metzler, 1971).

FEISE, ERNST. "Die Hochzeit des Mönchs von Conrad Ferdinand Meyer. Eine Formanalyse." In *Xenion: Themes, Forms and Ideas in German*

Literature, pp. 215–25 (Baltimore: Johns Hopkins University Press, 1950).

FLETCHER, BETTY LOEFFLER. "The 'Supreme Moment' as a Motif in C. F. Meyer's Poems." *Monatshefte* 42 (1950), 27–32.

FREY, ADOLF. *Conrad Ferdinand Meyer: Sein Leben und seine Werke* (Stuttgart: 4th ed., Cotta, 1925).

GUTHKE, KARL S. "C. F. Meyers Kunstsymbolik." In *Wege zur Literatur. Studien zur deutschen Dichtungs-und Geistesgeschichte,* pp. 187–204 (Bern: Francke, 1967).

D'HARCOURT, ROBERT. *Conrad Ferdinand Meyer: Sa vie, son oeuvre* (Paris: Alcan, 1913).

HARDAWAY, RICHARD TRAVIS. "Conrad Ferdinand Meyer's *Der Heilige* in Relation to Its Sources." *Publications of the Modern Language Association* 58 (1943), 245–63.

HENEL, HEINRICH. "Psyche. Sinn und Werden eines Gedichtes [Das Seelchen] von C. F. Meyer." *Deutsche Vierteljahresschrift für Literaturwissenschaft und Geistesgeschichte* 27 (1953), 358–86.

———. *The Poetry of Conrad Ferdinand Meyer* (Madison: University of Wisconsin Press, 1954).

———. "Erlebnisdichtung und Symbolismus." *Deutsche Vierteljahresschrift für Literaturwissenschaft und Geistesgeschichte* 32 (1958), 71–98.

———. *Gedichte Conrad Ferdinand Meyers: Wege ihrer Vollendung.* Deutsche Texte, vol. 8 (Tübingen: Niemeyer, 1962).

———. "Conrad Ferdinand Meyer: 'Lethe' and 'Stapfen,' " In *Die deutsche Lyrik: Von der Spätromantik bis zur Gegenwart,* edited by Benno von Wiese, pp. 217–29, 230–42 (Düsseldorf: Bagel, 1962).

HERZOG, VALENTIN. *Ironische Erzählformen bei Conrad Ferdinand Meyer dargestellt am Juerg Jenatsch.* Basler Studien zur deutschen Sprache und Literatur, vol. 42 (Bern: Francke, 1970).

HOF, WALTER. "Beobachtungen zur Funktion der Vieldeutigkeit in Conrad Ferdinand Meyers Novelle *Der Heilige.*" *Acta Germanica* 3 (1968), 207–23.

JACKSON, DAVID A. "Recent Meyer Criticism: New Avenues or cul-de-sac?" *Revue des langues vivantes* 34 (1968), 620–36.

———. "Conrad Ferdinand Meyer, *Huttens letzte Tage* and the Liberal Ideal." *Oxford German Studies,* no. 5 (1970), 67–89.

———. "Dante the Dupe in *Die Hochzeit des Mönchs.*" *German Life and Letters,* 25 (1971–1972), 5–15.

———. "Schadau, the Satirized Narrator, in C. F. Meyer's *Das Amulett.*" *Trivium* 7 (1972), 61–69.

———. "C. F. Meyer's *Die Richterin:* A Tussle with Tolstoi?" *Trivium* 9 (1974), 39–49.

———. *Conrad Ferdinand Meyer in Selbstzeugnissen und Bilddokumenten,* Rowohlts Bildmonographien (Hamburg: Rowohlt, 1975).

JENNINGS, LEE B. "The Ambiguous Explosion: C. F. Meyer's *Der Schuss von der Kanzel.*" *German Quarterly* 43 (1970), 210–22.

JESIORKOWSKI, KLAUS. "Die Kunst der Perspektive. Zur Epik Conrad Ferdinand Meyers." *Germanisch-romanische Monatsschrift,* n.s. 17 (1967), 398–416.

KIELHOLZ, ARTHUR. "C. F. Meyers Beziehungen zu Königsfelden." *Monatsschrift für Psychiatrie und Neurologie* 109 (1944), 257–89.

LUKACS, GEORG. "Conrad Ferdinand Meyer und der neue Typus des historischen Romans." In *Der historische Roman,* pp. 236–47 (Berlin: Aufbau 1955).

MARTINI, FRITZ. "Conrad Ferdinand Meyer." In *Deutsche Literatur im bürgerlichen Realismus,* 2d ed., pp. 801–44 (Stuttgart: Metzler, 1964).

MAYER, HANS. "Epische Spätzeit: C. F. Meyers *Jürg Jenatsch.*" In *Von Lessing bis Thomas Mann: Wandlungen der bürgerlichen Literatur in Deutschland,* pp. 317–37 (Pfullingen: Neske, 1959).

MAYNC, HARRY. *Conrad Ferdinand Meyer und sein Werk* (Frauenfeld: Huber, 1925).

MÜLLER, GÜNTHER. "Über das Zeitgerüst des Erzählens am Beispiel des *Jürg Jenatsch.*" *Deutsche Vierteljahresschrift für Literaturwissenschaft und Geistesgeschichte* 24 (1950), 1–32.

NILS, MARIA. *Betsy: Die Schwester Conrad Ferdinand Meyer's* (Frauenfeld: Huber, 1943).

OBERLE, WERNER. "Ironie im Werke C. F. Meyers." *Germanisch-romanische Monatsschrift,* n.s. 5 (1955), 212–22.

PESTALOZZI, KARL. "Tod und Allegorie in C. F. Meyers Gedichten." *Euphorion* 56 (1962), 300–20.

PLATER, EDWARD M. "The Banquet of Life: Conrad Ferdinand Meyer's *Die Versuchung des Pescara.*" *Seminar* 8 (1972), 88–98.

———. "The Figure of Dante in *Die Hochzeit des Mönchs.*" *Modern Language Notes* 90 (1975), 678–86.

REINHARDT, GEORGE W. "The Political Views of the Young Conrad Ferdinand Meyer with a Note on *Das Amulett.*" *German Quarterly* 45 (1972), 270–94.

SADGER, ISIDOR. *Konrad Ferdinand Meyer. Eine pathologisch-psychologische Studie* (Wiesbaden: Bergemann, 1908).

SANDBERG-BRAUN, BEATRICE. *Wege zum Symbolismus: Zur Entstehungsgeschichte dreier Gedichte Conrad Ferdinand Meyers.* Zürcher Beiträge zur deutschen Literatur-und Geistesgeschichte, vol. 32 (Zürich: Atlantis, 1969).

SCHIMMELPFENNIG, PAUL. "Meyer's Religion of the Heart. A Reevaluation of *Das Amuletts*" *Germanic Review* 47 (1972), 181—202.

SCHMID, KARL. "Conrad Ferdinand Meyer und die Grösse." In *Unbehagen im Kleinstaat,* pp. 13–110 (Zurich: Artemis, 1963).

SHAW, MICHAEL. "C. F. Meyer's Resolute Heroes." *Deutsche Vierteljahrsschrift für Literaturwissenschaft und Geistesgeschichte* 40 (1966), 360–90.

SILZ, WALTER. "C. F. Meyer: *Der Heilige.*" In *Realism and Reality: Studies in the German Novelle of Poetic Realism,* pp. 94–116 (Chapel Hill: University of North Carolina, 1954).

STAIGER, EMIL. "Das Spätboot. Zu Conrad Ferdinand Meyers Lyrik." In *Die Kunst der Interpretation,* pp. 237–73 (Zurich: Atlantis, 1955).

_____. "C. F. Meyer: 'Die tote Liebe,' " In *Meisterwerke deutscher Sprache aus dem 19. Jahrhundert* 4th ed., pp. 202–22 (Zurich: Atlantis, 1961).

SWALES, MARTIN, "Fagon's Defeat: Some Remarks on C. F. Meyer's *Das Leiden eines Knaben.*" *Germanic Review* 52 (1977), 29–43.

TUSKEN, LEWIS, "C. F. Meyer's *Der Heilige.* The Problem of Becket's Conversion." *Seminar* 7 (1971), 201–16.

WALKER, COLIN. "Unbelief and Martyrdom in C. F. Meyer's *Der Heilige.*" *German Life and Letters,* n.s. 21 (1967–1968), 111–22.

WEISHAAR, FRIEDRICH, *C. F. Meyers Angela Borgia.* Beiträge zur deutschen Literaturwissenschaft, vol. 30 (Marburg: Elwert, 1928).

WETZEL, HEINZ, "Der allzumenschliche Heilige: C. F. Meyers Novelle im Lichte von Nietzsches Gedanken zur Genealogie der Mor." *Etudes Germaniques* 30 (1975), 204–19.

VON WIESE, BENNO. "Conrad Ferdinand Meyer: *Die Versuchung des Pescara.*" In *Die deutsche Novelle von Goethe bis Kafka,* I, 250–67 (Düsseldorf: Bagel, 1964).

_____. "Conrad Ferdinand Meyer: *Die Hochzeit des Mönchs.*" In *Die deutsche Novelle,* II, 176–97.

WILLIAMS, W. D. *The Stories of C. F. Meyer* (Oxford: Oxford University Press, Clarendon Press, 1962).

YUILL, W. E. "Conrad Ferdinand Meyer." In *German Men of Letters,* edited by A. Nathan, I, 193–214. (London: Oswald Wolff, 1961).

ZÄCH, ALFRED. "Conrad Ferdinand Meyers Dichtung *Engelberg* und die Verserzählung des 19. Jahrhunderts." In *134. Neujahrsblatt zum Besten des Waisenhauses Zürich für 1971* (Zurich: Beer, 1971).

_____. *Conrad Ferdinand Meyer: Dichtkunst als Befreiung aus Lebenshemmnissen.* Wirkung und Gestalt, vol. 12 (Frauenfeld: Huber, 1973).

ZELLER, HANS. "Abbildung des Spiegelbildes. C. F. Meyers Verhältnis zur bildenden Kunst am Beispiel des Gedichts 'Der römische Brunnen.' " *Germanisch-romanische Monatsschrift,* n.s. 18 (1968), 72–80.

Index

172